The Ravens and the Prophet

Robert Weston

New Wine Press

New Wine Press
PO Box 17
Chichester
West Sussex PO20 6YB
England

ISBN: 1 874367 61 2

Typeset by CRB Associates, Reepham, Norfolk.
Printed in England by Clays Ltd, St Ives plc.

Acknowledgements

A number of people read the draft of this book at an early stage. I would like to single out in particular David Barrett (lecturer in English), Dr John Wolffe and David Jackson (both lecturers in history), Ros Dodd, Howard Porter, Paul Turton, Francis and Sally Prittie, Celia Redgrave, Nancy Brook and Jeremy Geere, who all devoted much time and thought to clarifying ideas and sharpening perspectives. I would also like to pay tribute to my father, John Weston, who, though not directly involved with this book, has helped me in so many ways to improve my writing skills. Biggest thanks of all to my wife Rosalind, for her numerous suggestions and endless patience.

My deepest appreciation also to Jackie Lines, Caroline Cadwallader, Judy Potter and Linda Jones for helping with the typing. You have brought this book to birth through all its many stages of development!

Contents

Introduction

Have you ever wondered how the Lord trained His servants for their hard and difficult callings? It is a great enigma. So many of the finest scriptural characters make their appearance on the pages of history 'fully-fledged' in their calling. There are tantalisingly few pointers to the hidden processes by which men such as Amos, Isaiah and Elijah were prepared for their ministry. My desire to learn more about the way God equips His people led me to take a closer look at the life of one of the greatest of all the prophets: Elijah the Tishbite.

Mention the name of Elijah and all manner of stirring images spring to mind: drought and fire, rank despair and triumphal faith, tyrants humbled and God exalted. True, we will find no book in Scripture named after Elijah: no grand schemes for reforming Temple Worship or mighty visions of the future. The number of times we see him 'in action' are not numerous, but the impact he made on friend and foe alike was deep and lasting. The few words we do hear from his lips resonate with fervour and insight. They span the intervening centuries with a clarion-call that demands our fullest attention.

The more we meditate on the life of this man whom God considered worthy to appear with the Lord Jesus on the Mount of Transfiguration, the more we will see that the whole tenor of Elijah's life, as well as the message he brought from his God, has much to teach our spiritually directionless generation. For if, at first, Elijah appears so full of holy fire that he towers above lesser mortals, a closer study will reassure us. Elijah's intimacy with God – and perhaps his weaknesses too – will surprise and inspire, rather than intimidate us.

I have endeavoured to communicate the heart of the message God entrusted to Elijah, because it contains a prophetic challenge for our own generation. I have been equally concerned that such an understanding should lead to a greater closeness to the Lord. The tone of this book, therefore, lies midway between the prophetic and the devotional, while the teaching ranges far beyond the life of the prophet himself. At the end of the day, I have been more concerned to communicate certain spiritual insights than to write a textual commentary. I offer no apology, therefore, for making so free a use of the Elijah narrative; it is an ideal springboard for developing our intimacy with God.

In Hidden Training with the Lord

Scripture offers us no direct glimpse of Elijah's early years, but we are given one clue. His first recorded utterance reveals that he 'stood before the Lord.' Hidden within these simple words lies the key not only for understanding Elijah's ministry, but for all who would follow in his footsteps.

Centuries before, the Lord had called Abraham His friend, spoken face to face with Moses, and described David as a man after his own heart. Now, in the obscurity of a remote mountain village, the Lord spent many years drawing Elijah deeper into His presence. To be designated as a mouthpiece for the Lord God Almighty is the highest of callings. Long before exposing him to the perils of public ministry, God had been at work, alerting him to the peril that faced the nation, scoring His burden deeply into his heart. Much hidden training thus preceded Elijah's rare, but exceedingly significant, forays onto the public stage.

To reach the mountain peaks, it is necessary first to pass through the foothills. In a sense, I have been more concerned in this book to explore the foothills that lead to the mountain ranges than with the summits themselves. This dimension of training will therefore be an important part of our study of what it means to live in the spirit and power of Elijah.

This book is an invitation to understand more of the God who supplies His people through ravens, and who speaks to us through prophets. The ravens symbolise God's imaginative provision for His people, just as the prophet represents the person who has learnt to express His heart.

So far as is possible, I have made each chapter complete in itself, whilst alluding in the references to a wealth of biblical texts, and other Christian literature. The prayers and meditations at the end of each section are a means of applying the teaching, and stimulating our devotional life. If the little word 'Selah' that we come across so often in the Psalms is, as many suppose it to be, an exhortation to 'Pause and Pray,' then let there be many such selahs in the course of reading this book. Who knows what the Lord may have to show us as we spend time in His presence?

It will be helpful to approach these times of reflection prayerfully. Take them slowly, and record any thoughts and insights as they come. It is my prayer that, long after you have closed the pages of this book, the wisdom and discernment that you glean through these times of reflection may remain as a precious and abiding part of your walk with the Lord.

Chapter 1

In the Courts of the Lord

'And Elijah the Tishbite, who was of the inhabitants of Gilead, said unto Ahab, "As the Lord the God of Israel lives, before whom I stand, there shall not be dew nor rain these years, but according to my word."'

(1 Kings 17:1 KJV)

Unexpected. That is as good a word as any to describe what happens when God reveals His heart to His people. From the Incarnation to the Resurrection, and on through the Ascension to Pentecost, God's dealings with mankind leave us reeling with surprise.

To follow the Lord's leading is the greatest of all adventures. Who but God would have thought of sending a lone man from the mountains to overthrow a royal dynasty? Like David, who was trained in a cave in order to reign in a palace, Elijah was reared in a school that was both sterner and yet sweeter than that to which we are accustomed. He spent the greater part of his life in rugged, inhospitable places, separated in heart and spirit from the prevailing compromise of his day. Elijah spoke into the heart of his generation with true perspectives and awesome authority, challenging the powers of darkness that had invaded the nation.

There can be few more dramatic scenes in the whole of

Scripture. Armed with nothing but the word the Lord had given him, a rugged man from the mountains burst into the court of King Ahab. There he proclaimed a truth no other man alive had had the courage to voice: that the God whom the playboy king had so recklessly ignored had declared a time of reckoning on the backslidden nation.

The future of Israel hung in the balance as Elijah strode onto the pages of recorded history. From a human point of view it looked foolhardy. Baal-worship had swept the nation, the prophets of the Lord had been silenced, and the cause of God appeared to have been all but defeated.

From heaven's perspective, things looked very different. God sent this man, whom He had trained in His own courts, to testify in the court of a corrupt king because He knew that the truth of His Word would first confront, and finally overthrow, the lies of the Baals, and the arrogance of the king.

Seeing with God's Eyes

Standing in the courts of the Lord, we see more clearly the reasons behind the outward events of our lives, and between spiritual cause and effect in society at large. We also discern the particular calling that is on our own lives.

In the presence of the Lord, Elijah had felt God's grief over the nation's backsliding. He had come to share His anger that the nation had dared to equate the Lord Almighty with the worthless Baals. His first public pronouncement imposed a judgement which would entail the most horrendous sufferings: a terrible drought would come upon the land.

Why did so drastic a sentence have to be visited on the nation? After all, it was barely a hundred years since the golden age of Israel, when David had ruled in the fear of the Lord. A quick glance at the preceding century is enough to reveal the main reasons. Solomon's infidelities had paved the way for the kingdom to be torn in two. Of the next seven kings who ruled the ten tribes, not one can be considered a faithful servant of the Lord.

The godly foundation that Samuel and David had developed was all but swept away. The speed at which the nation fell, first into spiritual indifference, and then into heathendom, is a stark reminder of how quickly a godly heritage can be eroded, when evil is allowed to spread unchallenged.

The nation had strayed so far from their God that nothing but judgement awaited it. When a still more ungodly man came to the throne, few were prepared to oppose him. Lewd and selfish by nature, Ahab became an unstoppable tyrant when marriage allied him to Jezebel, the scheming daughter of the king of the Sidonians. How the powers of darkness rejoiced to see the pair united! Jezebel imposed the worship of her alien gods and flooded the land with her own priests. An unprecedented storm of suffering fell on the heads of the true believers. Indeed, as Baal worship spread, it seemed for a time as though the worship of Yahweh was about to be driven once and for all from the face of the earth.[1]

As Elijah saw these things taking place, his heart burned within him. Tragically few others had the courage to stand against the new idolatries, and those who did were quickly silenced. So long as the economy was booming, and there was food on their table, people saw little point in risking their lives by speaking out. After all, since Yahweh Himself did not appear to be doing anything about the situation, most people preferred to stifle their conscience and pay at least lip service to the new gods.

Every generation presents us with similar temptations to compromise. In our own century, the example of many churches in Nazi Germany, and more recently in South Africa, Russia, Romania and China, reminds us how easy it is to reach a place of accommodation with evil – to say nothing of the myriad ways our hearts fall prey to the more sophisticated idolatries of materialism.

God sees all the dark forces in the world today, just as He did in the days when the Baals were worshipped in the land of Israel. He sees every act of injustice and He hears every cry of pain. He grieves that so few are prepared to declare war against this temptation to compromise, and to dedicate themselves instead to seeking Him.

Elijah would no more have welcomed the prospect of a prolonged drought than we would, but the Lord had revealed His will, and His servant had to be prepared to pay the cost involved in implementing it. Effectively, Elijah accepted that it was better for the nation to suffer hardship than to continue in its apostasy. The spiritual renewal which had not occurred in times of ease and prosperity might yet be brought about when harsher measures forced a rethink. As events turned out, his hope was not entirely disappointed.

The Sovereignty of God

Much of the beauty and power of Elijah's life comes from his willingness to embrace the clear directions God gave him. His obedience is, as it were, the foreground of his life. In the background, however, we can discern the sovereign actions of a God who cares very much what happens to His servants, and who ordains events accordingly.

When the Lord later commanded the ravens to bring Elijah meat, and the widow to feed him, neither the ravens nor the widow would have had any consciousness of being part of God's wider plan. This brings us face to face with something that is everywhere implicit, and often explicit, throughout the pages of Scripture: namely, the sovereignty of God.

When the enemy comes in like a flood, we need not despair: Satan has never been the ultimate master of any situation. God anticipates times of crises and prepares His witnesses accordingly. Thus Noah built his ark, Joseph gained favour in Pharaoh's court, Daniel became 'Prime Minister' of Babylon, and Esther Queen in Persia, all in order to avert the wholesale destruction of God's chosen people. Even in the darkest times, God has never ceased to undermine the stability of the evil forces, and to raise up His brightest lights: His Deborahs, Samuels and Elijahs.

As our understanding of God's sovereignty deepens, so it becomes no longer a mere doctrine, but a perceived reality. The events of our life, the people we meet, the places the Lord takes us to, and even the needs and delays we experience, all combine to play their part in helping us to develop a truly biblical approach to life.

The more we embrace this awareness of God having authority over matters beyond our control, the more we will enjoy freedom in worship, and confidence in our decision-making. Without such trust in His sovereign control (both over complex world affairs and the minutiae of our everyday lives) our hearts will often be doubt-ridden and anxiety-laden.

The finest truths of Scripture are not placed together in convenient charts and graphs. They are more like buried treasure that waits to be explored and pieced together. The more we study Scripture, the more clearly we perceive the God of first causes. We must look beyond purely economic or military reasons to understand that it was the Lord who brought Israel up from Egypt, the Philistines from Crete and the Syrians from Kir[2] – just as it was He who delivered Israel from the tyranny of the Baals – and us from our own many scrapes!

It is especially in the books of the prophets that we meet the God who declares, 'I am (this or that) and I will (do this or that).' It is He who raises men up and who casts them down again.[3] Here is an understanding that will impart a sense of imminence to our reading of the Bible. Tempted though we may be to skip over many of the prophetic oracles in search of more familiar pastures, a closer study of these passages will repay the effort a thousand times over. Not only will our understanding of the heart and character of God deepen, but we will increasingly discern spiritual meaning and patterns behind the shifting episodes of life.

God calls us into His courts not only to deepen our relationship with Him, but also to show us how He feels about things. His ways are as varied as His means, but by one means or another, He will develop understanding in our hearts, fill the ordinary with new meaning and turn sight into insight. In short, we will begin to see with His eyes.

The Supreme Court

Scripture reveals how willing God is to show us not only what He is doing, but also why. From the moment the Lord shared His hidden counsel with Abraham, right through the writings of the prophets until the revelations He entrusted to John on the island of Patmos, we find God revealed as the One who is sovereign over men and nations alike – but who 'confides' in those who fear Him, taking the upright into His confidence.[4]

Beyond all human courts, where rulers exercise their authority, Scripture alludes to the existence of a supreme heavenly court. This is where the decrees are issued that affect both life and eternity.[5] The Lord draws us into this court in order to help us to see with His eyes, and to understand what is on His heart.

All true prophets have stood in the courts of the Lord. Isaiah and Daniel were but two of the most prominent who 'eavesdropped' on the worship of heaven, and thereby discovered more of God's commission on their own life. As they saw the Lord seated in His court, they were granted insight into the workings, as well as the worship, of this heavenly assembly.[6]

It was not every day that these prophets experienced great visions. Those they did receive are, as it were, the recorded highlights of their lives, and their deepest understanding of the ways of heaven. When they saw the Lord seated in His court, for instance, they realised with a fresh immediacy that God does not merely watch events on Earth from Heaven: He directs their outworking.

When Daniel overheard specific decrees and judgements being issued in the throne room of God, he perceived that world empires are allowed to rule only by heaven's decree. The power of evil men would, in due time, be stripped from them. He also understood that, in some mysterious way, God incorporates the intercessions of His people into His decision-making process.[7]

The Hebrew word that is used to describe this court is *sôdh.*[8] Since this word means both 'council' (as in a council chamber) and 'counsel', the term embraces not only a circle of intimate friends, but also the particular affairs discussed between them. From this court flow mercy and judgement, even as friendship and understanding develop in our hearts as we draw near to the King of Kings.

The Prophet's Task

From time immemorial it has been the function of the prophet to put the trumpet to his lips and to declare what he has seen and heard in the courts of the Lord. The word of God must be made explicit, because generalities usually fail to convince men of their sin.

Centuries beforehand, Moses had steeled himself to enter Pharaoh's court. Now, Elijah knew that the moment had come to take his message of judgement to the king. It does not take much imagination to realise that the role of the prophet is a hard rather than a glamorous one. Because the prophet is called to 'uproot and tear down' as well as to 'build and to plant', he (or she) will inevitably face misunderstanding and opposition.[9]

A.G. Gardener wrote,

> 'When a prophet is deified, his message is lost. The prophet is only useful so long as he is stoned as a public nuisance, calling us to repentance, disturbing our comfortable routines, breaking our respectable idols and shattering our sacred conventions.'

So high is this calling, and so solemn its outworkings, that God has to go to extreme lengths to prepare people to execute this ministry in humility of spirit.[10]

The Drought Decreed

It is a sublimely fitting irony that God should choose a rugged man from the mountains to be the one to take His message to the fineries of Ahab's court. Elijah's task was outwardly as daunting as the latter-day mission of John the Baptist to denounce Herod's extra-marital indulgences. King Ahab, like Nebuchadnezzar after him, would have to learn the hard way that all the pomp of earthly trappings could avail him naught against a decree that was issued from the throne room of heaven.

Boldly refusing to allow any fear of the consequences to water down his message, Elijah dared to predict the unpredictable: a drought of unspecified duration would afflict the land. The sentence had been pronounced, and no further rain would fall until he, Elijah, so decreed it.

The drought was a rebuke to the nation, a direct rebuttal of Ahab's complacent assumption that all was well under his rule, and a challenge to the people to consider why their God had had to send it. If Elijah had not brought this specific revelation concerning the forthcoming drought, people would have been quick to find some other way of explaining it away. Perhaps, in those superstitious days, the drought might have been blamed on bad spirits. In today's terminology it would doubtless be attributed to the Greenhouse Effect! The prophetic declaration marked God's intended action, and His decree would not be revoked, unless or until it was stayed by mercy, through the repentance of His people.

Reflections

To see with God's eyes is an enormous privilege. It enables us to see people with the Lord's eyes of love, and to understand issues with a greater degree of clarity. It can be exceedingly painful, however, for we will come face to face with the same sins which merited God's judgement in Elijah's day, and we must respond accordingly.

> *'Hear and pay attention, do not be arrogant, for the Lord has spoken. Give glory to the Lord your God before He brings the darkness, before your feet stumble on the darkening hills . . . But if you do not listen, I will weep in secret because of your pride; my eyes will weep bitterly, overflowing with tears.'*[11]

Selah

Dear Lord, as I meditate on Elijah's life, help me to grasp more clearly how You feel about Your world. Thank You that You sent Elijah to Ahab's court in the power of the Spirit. Thank You that he did not hold back from following You there. I ask that You will draw me closer to Your heart, and set me free from my own preoccupations and willingness to compromise, so that I may see with Your eyes, and be more open to Your leading. In Jesus' name, Amen.[12]

References

1. cf 1 Kings 18:13
2. Acts 17:28; cf Amos 3:6b, 9:7; Psalm 94:8–10
3. e.g. Isaiah 45:6–11
4. Psalm 25:14; Proverbs 3:32; cf Genesis 18:17–21; Amos 3:6b; Psalm 94:8–10; Isaiah 45:7. It is worth adding that the Lord often reveals these reasons some considerable time after they have happened, as it were interpreting them to us.
5. Job 1:6ff; Daniel 7:9–27; Zechariah 3:1ff; cf Jeremiah 23:18–22
6. Isaiah 6:3, 6–8; Daniel 7:9ff
7. Daniel 7:9–27 but see also chapters 8–12
8. Daniel 7:9ff
9. Hosea 9:7–8, 10:2 We shall be looking at some of the principles involved in handling a word from the Lord in the chapter 'The Prophetic Ministry'.
10. John and Paula Sandford have valuable insights into the training that is necessary to equip us for the prophetic ministry in their book *The Elijah Task* (Logos)
11. Jeremiah 13:15–17; cf Joel 2:12–17; Zephaniah 2:1–3
12. You may find it helpful to spend some time in the near future re-reading at least one of the books of the prophets. Study how the prophets each found their own way of presenting the Lord's burden. For example, Malachi used dramatic dialogue between God and His people, Amos exposed the sins of the neighbouring nations, before going on to show that the chosen people were no better themselves; Hosea was led to marry an unfaithful partner, as a symbol of Israel's infidelity, Habakkuk wrestled with the violence that surrounded him, while Ezekiel used dramatic actions to get his message across to the people. The understanding that will accrue from such an in-depth study of the books of the prophets will go a long way towards developing a truly prophetic understanding of life.

Chapter 2

The Hidden Life

Elijah was under no illusions. He knew full well that his words would make him the target of Ahab's wrath, and the scapegoat for the tens of thousands who would suffer as a result of the drought. Elijah had no fall-back plan to make good his escape – but he appears never to have doubted that help would be given him when it was most needed.

> *'Then the word of the Lord came to Elijah: "Leave here, turn eastwards and hide in the ravine of Kerith, east of the Jordan. You will drink from the brook, and I have ordered the ravens to feed you there." So Elijah did what the Lord had told him. He went to the Kerith ravine, east of the Jordan, and stayed there.'* (1 Kings 17:2–5)

In the nick of time, God did indeed speak to His servant – but what a strange word it was! Withdraw to the back of beyond and be fed by ravens beside a stream? It can hardly be termed a glamorous start to a preaching career – let alone a fitting reward for a mission faithfully accomplished. In the service of the Kingdom, however, obedience precedes understanding.

True, we are wise to check and double-check every leading we believe to be of God, but to hold back when God has told us clearly to do something implies that we do not trust Him. An irresolute mind opens the way for all manner of doubts and misgivings. The powers of darkness find it much harder to torment a steadfast and resolute mind.[1]

What the Lord shows us will often fight against our natural understanding. Since 'Cherith' (or 'Kerith') means a 'drought', then surely this, of all brooks, must be prone to dry up when the rains failed? How tempting it must have been to move on and preach God's word in other towns and villages. Yet Elijah dared not disobey. If he ignored this call to go into hiding, he would become just one more victim of Ahab's vicious campaign against the followers of Yahweh.

Quite apart from the sheer necessity of hiding His hunted servant, the Hebrew text provides us with a clue as to God's deeper purposes in telling Elijah to 'hide' by the brook Cherith. The word means to 'absent oneself' rather than just to seek concealment. To preach and pray for others is to bring the peace and beauty of the Lord into broken and disordered lives. To do so repeatedly is exceedingly demanding work, and the Lord needed to fill His servant afresh with His power.

Men may think that the limelight is the place to do their most important work, but prophets have a responsibility not only to the affairs of this world, but to the interests of God's Kingdom. Scripture makes it plain that the Lord accomplishes much of His best, and most lasting, work in unseen places, through hidden faithfulness. There was much the Lord could do in Elijah's life only because He had him on his own.

The Wisdom of God's Foolishness

God's wisdom is so incomparably higher than our own that it often appears to be mere foolishness.[2] Just as the Lord chose David ahead of his apparently better-suited brothers, so He continues to choose the most unlikely people today to further His Kingdom, using those who are most aware of their weakness. Who but God would have thought of sending a young oboe player to the walled city of Hong Kong to minister to some of the world's most needy drug addicts? Who else, for that matter, could have kept Jackie To (Pullinger) faithful to her calling through the long 'hidden' years during which she saw no fruit from her ministry? Yet who today has not heard of the amazing work God has done through her?

Instinctively, men fear weakness, and take out all manner of insurance policies to protect themselves from trouble. Scripture reveals a remarkably different emphasis in which the obscure are exalted, and times of trouble become the means by which the Lord fulfils His purposes.[3]

The Welsh miner, Rees Howells, is a striking example of one who yielded to this call to the hidden life. After some years of fruitful ministry, God asked him to leave his job as a miner and to withdraw from his popular preaching ministry in order to spend more time alone with Himself. It was a costly decision in every way. Many failed to perceive the leading of the Spirit and came to the utterly mistaken conclusion that he had backslidden.

Concerning this period in his life, his biographer wrote,

> 'At first the world affected him, but in the end it was he who affected the world.'[4]

When the Lord released him again to minister in public, thousands came to faith through the missions he conducted in Africa. All could then enjoy the fruit of his obedience.

In the light of the world-wide ministries the Lord entrusted to these people, how grateful we can be that they did not lose sight of their original calling, and give up during the years of apparent fruitlessness. Beyond the seeming waste and foolishness lay the Master's hidden purposes.

I believe that many of us have not progressed into a

deeper maturity in the faith because we have not sufficiently yielded ourselves to the Lord. We are still at the stage of making bargains with God: 'If You will do this, then I will do that...' Wisdom lies in letting Him have His way, for He knows exactly what He is planning to do.

If the thought of making such a complete surrender appears daunting, then consider the alternative. Could anything be more foolish than to hold back on the Lord who has our very best interests at heart? The Lord never takes anything from our lives without putting something infinitely richer back in its place. May we be stripped of our inclination to rebel whenever God calls 'time' on something that has meant a lot to us.

Reflections

> *'The eyes of the Lord range throughout the earth to strengthen those whose hearts are fully committed to Him ... "Who is the one who will devote himself to be close to Me?"'*[5]

Either from the Bible, or from firsthand acquaintance, make a list of men and women who have been called aside by God in order that He could fulfil greater purposes through them at a later date. What does this have to say about God's priorities?

Selah

> Lord, I long to be more in Your company. Take me beyond the realm of needing to be needed, and into a place of greater intimacy with Yourself. Still the restlessness of my soul, and lead me into a deeper relationship with You in the hidden places. In Jesus' name, Amen.

References

1. See James 1:6–8
2. 1 Samuel 16:11–13; cf 1 Corinthians 1:18–29
3. cf 1 Corinthians 2:2–3, 4:9–10; 2 Corinthians 1:8–9, 6:4, 11:30, 12:9–10
4. *Rees Howells, Intercessor* (Lutterworth Press)
5. 2 Chronicles 16:9; Jeremiah 30:21. Concerning this call to deepen our devotional life, Richard Foster's book *Prayer – Finding the Heart's True Homeland* (Hodder) is an outstanding introduction to the contemplative life. So too is *The Imitation of Christ*, by Thomas à Kempis, the best-selling Christian book of all time after the Bible. (Highland Books have produced a modern translation.)

Chapter 3

By the Brook Cherith

'So Elijah did what the Lord had told him. He went to the Kerith ravine, east of the Jordan, and stayed there.' (1 Kings 17:5)

To the functionally minded, Elijah's prolonged stay by the brook Cherith looks like a waste of a promising life. Here was the nation's foremost prophet, eking out an existence in an isolated nowhere. What chance had he now of addressing king and court, or of leading a spiritual revival? But God's ways are not ours. The time had not yet come to send him back to lock horns again with Ahab and Jezebel.

By leading His servant away from the familiar mountains of Gilead, and from the challenge of exercising a prophetic ministry in a hostile setting, God was offering Elijah not only an extended period of rest from his labours, but a precious opportunity to deepen his closeness to Himself. The stresses Elijah faced here would be of a totally different kind.

Most of us depend far more than we realise for our spiritual well-being on our relationships with each other. Yet here was Elijah, a leader with nobody to lead, and a preacher with nobody to preach to. That alone would be enough to give most ministers an outsize crisis of identity!

It is infinitely harder than it sounds to continue to seek God when we have no obvious goal in sight. To be able to abide for considerable periods of time in His presence, without allowing fears to drag us down, or passing excitements to turn our head, is a great achievement.

At Cherith, God slowed Elijah's life down to walking pace. The months God's chosen prophet spent, whiling away long hot days by a remote wadi, stand in sharp contrast not only to the superficial frenzy of the court he had left behind, but also to the way most of us lead our lives. It begs an important question for us adrenalin addicts of the twentieth century: how can Elijah's sojourn by the brook inspire us to change the speed at which we lead our own lives?

Is there any way we can avoid living at so furious a pace that we cause ourselves indigestion and insomnia? Are we at risk of becoming a time-bomb on legs? Are not at least some of our stress-points self-induced? We would do well to examine these things, and to make room for the things we really need in life – time, companionship, recreational activities, compassion and so on. They may be nearer to us than we had imagined.

Bringing our souls into balance requires serious choices. A German proverb warns, 'Wer hat Wahl hat Qual' (whoever has choice has pain). Our starting point is clear enough: we are concerned to follow our Lord's example and do only what we see our Heavenly Father doing.[1] Working this principle out in practice, however, will stretch us to the utmost.

Elijah's options may have been more restricted than our own, but he too would have experienced strong temptations to disobey God by going somewhere else. It is greatly to his credit that Elijah stayed where he was. After all, would we be able to seek God resolutely if we were faced by the daily possibility of being mauled by wild animals?

Almost anything is bearable, provided we know how long

it is going to last. Yet Elijah had no way of knowing how long God intended to keep him by the brook. In the meantime he would have the decidedly dubious privilege of being provided for by ravens – an unlikely means of support, but well chosen in that they would be far less likely to betray Elijah's whereabouts than a fellow human being.

It is an almost universal law that when earthly doors are barred to us, the gates of heaven will swing open. So far from allowing Elijah to perish in this remote no-man's land, the Lord sent ravens to bring him food, just as He had met the Israelites in the desert, and supplied them with manna from heaven.

We can imagine that, as month succeeded uneventful month, Elijah became more practised at seeking the Lord. Although nothing happened outwardly, God was far from inactive. Though he had no way of knowing it, Elijah's most fruitful period of ministry still lay ahead of him. Meanwhile, there was no point sending his blood pressure soaring by worrying whether the ravens would remember to come on the morrow – or whether tomorrow might be the day the Lord released him from his enforced withdrawal. God was preparing him to carry still greater burdens by teaching him to live from one day to the next.

Soaked in the Word

Dietrich Bonhoeffer passed a telling comment on the way society works when he wrote,

> 'We have no proper understanding of the need for scriptural proof. We hear arguments "from life" and "from experience" put forward as the basis for the most crucial decisions, but the argument of Scripture is missing. And this authority would, perhaps, point in exactly the opposite direction.'[2]

The word of the Lord was so powerful in Elijah's life because its truth lived in his heart. In the days before the printed word, man used his memory to better effect than he does today. We can be sure Elijah would have taken the trouble to memorise those portions of the Word of God which were then in existence, and that he spent a great deal of his time by the brook Cherith in prayerful meditation.

Precisely because so much of what I am sharing in this book may appear to be 'experience-oriented', it is important to stress that we are not equipped to embark on understanding the prophetic calling (or the contemplative life either for that matter) until the truths of the Bible saturate our mind, shape our thinking and check our impulses. The Lord 'tunes' our heart, and increases our wisdom as we study His word verse by verse.

Much though we will benefit by reading large chunks of Scripture (and it is important for us to understand the whole counsel of God) many of us will derive at least as much profit from taking just a short passage, or even a single sentence, and savouring it to the point where its truth begins to live in our heart. The Psalmist tells us it is the entrance of God's Word which gives light and imparts understanding.[3] Like Mary we can ponder its significance, and wait for the Lord to make the interpretation and its application plain to us. Thus we learn not just about God, but of God Himself directly, through the help of His Holy Spirit.

Take a passage from the Bible, and read the text through several times, preferably out loud, to let its truth penetrate your heart. Try to imagine the scene, first from the perspective of the speaker, then from that of the hearer, the bystanders and so on. You will soon find yourself identifying with the joys and sorrows of earlier pilgrims, and discovering fresh perspectives and implications as you do so.

The word of God assumes a new depth once it is stored in the heart. Many great musicians and actors feel that they can only really bring a piece of music or drama to life when they have committed it to memory. This is not the way most of us operate – but perhaps we ought to. A Chinese believer, imprisoned for twenty three years, and deprived of access to the Bible, testified on his release how greatly the many passages of Scripture he had committed to memory as a young man had sustained him during those long years. How much Scripture would we be able to recall if put to such a test? Most of us do not have bad memories: we simply have undeveloped ones!

We can enjoy so much that Elijah was deprived of. We have access to Christian literature that distils for us the wisdom of the centuries, as well as every possible aid to Bible study. A little imagination, combined with a few good reference books, can lead us into all manner of fruitful lines of study. The possibilities are endless. Whatever form of reading plan we adopt, however, should cause us to read God's word until we receive His marching orders for the day. For the Bible is not so much a book to be studied, and a set of doctrines to be learnt by rote, as food for our mind and manna for our soul.

A Cherith Week

Western spirituality has long tended to focus on positive action: 'What God has done for me and what I must do for God.' The result has been that we live our lives at break-neck speed, constantly acting and reacting to stressful situations. I have increasingly come to the conclusion that most well-established Christians are less in need of the additional teaching their mind has taught them to expect, than a deeper awareness of the Lord Himself. Times apart can greatly strengthen this.

Many of us will experience great blessing if we can manage to set aside a week alone, with nothing to do except to seek the Lord. Whether we spend it in a retreat centre, or in our own house, the important thing is to set ourselves entirely free from our day-to-day responsibilities. We are not retreating from the world: we are advancing towards our Father.

Such an immersion in the Lord's presence can have a revolutionary effect on our relationship with Him. In the stillness and the silence we learn to seek the Lord, face ourselves, and, in the process, we overcome many strongholds of darkness. In retrospect, we realise that such weeks have permanently altered many of our perspectives and priorities.

Reflections

I believe that God was showing us a spiritual pattern when He took Elijah away from civilisation. Cherith was a trysting place as well as a hide-out: an appointed rendezvous where lovers meet. As such, like Elijah's later pilgrimage to Horeb, it challenges us to consider the benefits of setting aside our own 'Cherith' weeks.

What steps are you taking to allow yourself extended 'time out' with God? Practical measures will need to be taken even for a single day away, let alone a whole week, but the effort involved will repay itself many times over.

Selah

> Lord, help me to make the effort to spend more time in Your presence. Quiet the worries of my mind, and enable me to receive Your Word. Develop my memory, and fill it with the truths of Your Word. Protect me from all distractions and deceptions as I seek to go deeper in Your presence. Help me love, embrace and cherish silence, until I find You in the still place of my heart. In Jesus' name, Amen.

References

1. John 5:19
2. *Life Together*, Dietrich Bonhoeffer (SCM), p. 39. Sadly, this same criticism could also be applied to large parts of the Church.
3. Psalm 119:130 (KJV)

Chapter 4

The Shrinking Brook

'And it came to pass after a while that the brook dried up, because there had been no rain in the land.'

(1 Kings 17:7 KJV)

For several long months Elijah lived in enforced seclusion. Blessed though he was by the Lord's presence, this must also have been a time of great tension. Not only did he have to wait day after day for the ravens to bring him food, but he would also have been ever conscious of 'Ahab the Vengeful' scouring the country in search of him. As if these pressures were not enough, Elijah now faced a still more imminent danger: his supply of water was beginning to dry up.

Whichever way you look at it, Elijah's predicament was extreme. The Lord had said that Elijah would drink from the brook, but He had not promised to send any rain – and the Cherith brook was drying up. Neither had He given him any idea what He was going to do to provide for him when it did.

As the full weight of his predicament settled on him, any hope of being of use again to man or nation must have seemed like a distant mirage. All too acutely he would have felt the poverty of his food, the harshness of his environment and the monotony of his days. Everything had been bearable so long as the brook flowed – it had even been a privilege to make do with so little – but who can live without water?

As Elijah watched the brook shrinking, it would have been easy to have indulged in bitter thoughts towards God. Like Isaiah he might have shouted out: *'Truly, You are a God who hides Himself!'*[1] Yet Elijah did not waste time and energy blaming God for his plight, and neither should we, when we find ourselves faced with equally incomprehensible and life-threatening situations.

In many ways, the further we go with the Lord the higher our expectations become. Buoyed up by past deliverances, triumphant faith reaches out to believe for more than is humanly possible. But what happens when we step out in obedience, only to find circumstances contradicting all we believe God has promised?

These occasions can be exceedingly painful – especially when we sense other people looking askance at our confusion. This is a time for doing what the Lord gives us to do from one day to the next, and for not yielding to disturbing thoughts. Sooner or later, a fresh set of circumstances will unfold, further revelation be granted, and all that has been promised will come to pass.[2]

Since we may, from time to time, experience just such a sequence of promise and delay in our own lives, I would like to share a spiritual pattern we have noted on a number of occasions. (I say 'pattern' advisedly because I do not believe in formulas!)

We find ourselves confronted with a serious difficulty which hangs heavily over us – much as Elijah faced a shortage of water. When God finally speaks to us about it, we are both thrilled and relieved. What He says, however, may still leave us feeling bewildered, because we can see no way by which His word can be fulfilled.

We can summarise this process thus:

> Difficulty (with all its accompanying temptations to Despondency) gives way to Discernment. When the initial Delirium has worn off, however, we are still left with such a Dilemma that it leads to a further period of Darkness. Provided we do not open the gate to Doubt or Disillusionment, we will live to experience God's Deliverance – to our utmost Delight!

Don't Panic!

If we have ever known the temptation to abandon a project too soon, or to come home early from a retreat, we can imagine that Elijah must have experienced an almost overwhelming longing to head for home, and to take his chance with the king's hostility.

As he looked around the drearily familiar terrain that bordered his dried-up wadi, Elijah must have been sorely tempted to go foraging for food and water. There is a sense in which doing almost anything feels better than doing nothing – and thirst can make sensible men do the most desperate things. In far less testing circumstances than those which Elijah faced, have we not rushed to seek solutions to our predicaments with all the mature reflection of a distraught chicken?

There is no need to panic; God is closer than we think. Elijah knew the Lord had directed him to the brook Cherith, and he dared not desert his post without a fresh commission. If the Lord was closing down this means of support, then He would surely open up another. Resolutely refusing to run away, Elijah waited for the Lord to show him what to do next. Would He again cause water to pour from a rock as He had done for Moses? Not on this occasion! God has different solutions for each dilemma that we face, and we can never afford to rely on yesterday's guidance.

Faith must always be put to the test.[3] The Lord does not hide the enormity of a situation from our eyes. It is entirely consistent with the way He works that He allowed Elijah to watch the water-level shrinking from one day to the next before telling him what He was going to do about it.

Perhaps it is not surprising if God feels a long way off during these times when the stream of our life is drying up. The Lord often 'hides' His purpose from us during these periods, for the simple reason that if we knew what was going to happen in advance, we would be tempted to dwell more on the promises He had given than to remain in an attitude of humble dependency.

Neither will the Lord allow Himself to be limited by our expectations. The sentence of drought had been decreed, and if Elijah had chosen to believe that this particular stream would be spared, then he would have been deceiving himself – and deception makes us less well equipped to handle reality. Do not so many of our mistakes stem from adding our own interpretation to what God has said?

All we can do during these times of drought is to rest on His faithfulness, and to cry out to Him to fulfil His purposes. Has He ever let His loved ones down? The very 'dryness' we experience can serve to sharpen our longing and to purify our prayer.

The Sinai Blues

Humanly speaking, Elijah had much to fear. This man of the mountains knew far better than we do that ravens are members of the crow family. These scavengers are hardly noted for their generosity in distributing food to passing prophets. But just imagine how unhappy Elijah would have been if he had spent all his time worrying whether the ravens would arrive the next day. Where was their seemingly inexhaustible secret store of food? Or, in modern terminology, what would happen if some trigger-happy farmer fetched his shotgun and made himself a raven pie? And just what was going on back home while he was stuck in the middle of nowhere?

It is a sad indictment that we, who are the only people on Earth who can really afford to be joyful, so rarely are. Inordinate passions weigh us down and make it hard for us to smile: fear, which robs us of our inner peace; avarice, that can never have enough; ambition, that knows no limit. These are the emotions that inflame and bewitch the heart.

As the brook dried up, Elijah was being reminded in the most direct way possible that he could not afford to look to earthly sources for his ultimate security. We are pilgrims on the way, and we must be careful not to put our roots down too deeply in the affairs of this world.[4]

If the Lord sometimes allows us, like Elijah, to watch the stream of our earthly provision drying up before He shows us what He is going to do about it, this is, in one sense, only to highlight the contrast between our helplessness and His all-sufficiency. He who sent us out will provide us with all we need to make it to the end of our journey. His commissions contain His hidden provision – and He will never allow us to be tested beyond our ability to endure.

We may not be responsible for the circumstances that assail us, but we assuredly are for our response. I cannot speak for you, but I am only too aware of my propensity to fall into 'moan-mode' whenever the going gets sufficiently tough, or when I am feeling tired or anxious. We must try at all costs during these times of uncertainty to avoid succumbing to the sin which plagued the children of Israel during their long years in the wilderness – the grumbling spirit that I have christened 'The Sinai Blues'.

If you are anything like me, you probably waste a great deal of mental energy worrying about things the Lord already has in hand. It is rather like driving with one foot on the brake. We cannot change the past, but we can easily ruin a perfectly good present by worrying about the future. Given how inclined most of us are to this, it may sound harsh to say that worry is a sin – so let me try putting it the other way round: it is not a sin not to worry!

Time and again we suffer needless heartache because we cannot see how He is going to handle some dilemma that is beyond our control. The Lord is not anxious: He knows what He is doing, and He wants our hearts to be made stronger, rather than harder, through the circumstances which happen to us.

Scattering our Fears

Jesus taught His disciples so much about the nature and the power of faith because He wants us to respond to our problems in the same spirit of faith and trust with which He Himself met difficulties. In the Hebrew text of the verse, *'You will keep in perfect peace him whose mind is steadfast,'* the word 'peace' is repeated twice. 'Perfect peace' captures the flavour beautifully. The reference to the 'mind' reminds us that this is where our real warfare is centred: in the 'mind-field!'[5]

Most of us find it easier to trust the Lord for our salvation, and even for our sanctification, than we do to meet the daily difficulties of life. To determine to trust the Lord, rather than to fret, marks a sign of real spiritual growth. Brother Lawrence wrote,

> 'All things are possible to him who believes; they are less difficult to him who hopes; they are still easier to him who loves; they are even easier to him who practises all three virtues.'[6]

Christians who have learnt the secret of praising God during times of testing and distress will be far less prone to those faith-crippling bouts of the 'but what if . . .' mentality.

It is impossible to praise God and succumb to negative thoughts at one and the same time. It is the best and fastest way to remind ourselves that all things do indeed work together for the good of those who love the Lord.[7] By praise and faith we can overcome every giant that stands in our way, and take every thought captive.

Frank Boreham illustrates this principle with a telling parable. He suggests that, like the virgins, there are two kinds of bird: the foolish and the wise. Foolish are the birds who allow the scarecrow to deter them – wise are the ones who realise that the very presence of a scarecrow points to juicy pickings!

Although we may feel as though all we had hoped and longed for is further away than ever, God knows both what He must do, and when He must do it, in order to lead us on. He will not fail to send us His 'ravens' as we set out at His bidding.

Do not be too upset, therefore, when circumstances appear almost overwhelmingly difficult: God is trusting us to keep going. Say rather,

> I am here by His will in this painful time of affliction, when ill-health dogs me, friends forsake me, and when the forces of the world and of darkness are pressing in. He is here with me, and since He is always more faithful to me than I deserve, He will deliver me from this dilemma, to the glory of His name.

It is such a joy when the Lord overcomes obstacles for us – or even when we discover that the focus of our anxiety has been an imaginary fear. Like the two Marys, who made their way to the tomb worrying how they were going to roll the stone away, only to find that it had already been rolled aside for them, so we will find that God already has in mind what He is going to do to help us.

Reflections

The Lord who was with Elijah is also with us, even though it may feel for the moment as though everything around us is shrinking rather than expanding. Commit a 'drying brook' situation to the Lord now. It may be a business or an organisation that is struggling to make ends meet, or a friendship that is under strain. Ask the Lord to pour out His mercy on it – and to keep the people involved from falling into the 'Sinai Blues!'

Selah

> Lord, I praise You that nothing is impossible for those who have faith in You. Forgive me that I have looked more at the water level shrinking from day to day than I have at You. Here and now I resolve that the very next time a situation occurs which looks as though Your purposes are going to be defeated, I will trust You to work it out in such a way as to bring You great glory. In Jesus' name, Amen.

References

1. Isaiah 45:15
2. There may be occasions, of course, when we will need to eat humble pie and admit we had been mistaken in supposing that it was the Lord who had led us in a particular direction. Sadly, some are too proud, and some too stubborn, to retrace their steps. Hanging on grimly to what they mistakenly believe to have been a word from the Lord, they bulldoze others into their lopsided way of thinking.
3. Moses and the Israelites had to watch the Egyptian army drawing ever closer in hot pursuit before the Lord disclosed His wonderful plan to bring His people through the Red Sea (Exodus 14:9ff). You will probably be able to think of other biblical examples.
4. Hebrews 13:14
5. Isaiah 26:3. The word 'mind' is translated 'imagination' in the Revised Version. This is a useful reminder for those of us who know how

much damage can be done when we allow our imagination to dwell on thoughts and images which weaken our will.

6. Brother Lawrence – *The Practice of the Presence of God*
7. Romans 8:28; cf 1 Thessalonians 5:18; cf Ephesians 2:6–10. It is helpful to remember that psychologists reckon that more than 80% of our fears have no substance in reality.

Chapter 5

Strange Guidance

'Then the word of the Lord came to Elijah: "Go at once to Zarephath of Sidon and stay there. I have commanded a widow in that place to supply you with food." So Elijah went to Zarephath. When he came to the town gate, a widow was there gathering sticks. He called to her and asked, "Would you bring me a little water in a jar so I may have a drink?" As she was going to get it, he called, "And bring me, please, a piece of bread."

"As surely as the Lord your God lives," she replied, "I don't have any bread – only a handful of flour in a jar and a little oil in a jug. I am gathering a few sticks to take home and make a meal for myself and my son, that we may eat it – and die." (1 Kings 17:8–12)

What a joy it must have been for Elijah to hear again the Lord's direction for his life! As the implications of the word became clearer, however, and the still small voice fainter, bewilderment returned, like a besetting cloud of flies. Here he was, eagerly awaiting the call to return to release the rain in Israel, being summoned to the kingdom of Queen Jezebel's father. It was like asking a Christian to go and live in Mecca!

A lesser man would have balked at so strange a command. What could one man do against such fearsome odds? True, life in the Spirit was never designed for those who look too much to their own security, but sending Israel's finest prophet out of the country altogether hardly looks the ideal solution for overthrowing Baal worship. But the Lord was more interested, for the moment, in deepening His work in Elijah's life than in sending him back to challenge the Baals.

The Place of Refining

There are few things most of us fear so much as losing face.[1] The Lord's instructions to Elijah must have sounded like a death-knell to his pride. To be told that God intended to provide for him through a woman was doubly humiliating in a culture which inhibited men from receiving anything from the hand of any woman – let alone a widow.[2]

Seventy difficult and dangerous desert miles separated Elijah from the aptly named township of Zarephath: 'The Place of the Smelting Furnace'. It was a prophetic indication of the refining that lay ahead.

Allegorically, Zarephath represents an important stage in God's dealings with us. There are certain things the Lord can only accomplish by changing our circumstances. Perhaps many of us can identify with some plants that F.B. Meyer, a celebrated preacher and writer of the last century, once came across. They were the most luxurious shrubs he had ever seen, and his enquiries revealed that they owed their splendour to having been continually transplanted. So far from weakening the plants, the repeated replantings had actually served to strengthen them.

The Lord values our union with Himself so highly that He is quite prepared to shake all that can be shaken if this will succeed in purging us of our dross. It is both a comfort and a challenge, therefore, that the Lord Jesus tells us,

'I am the true vine and my Father is the gardener. He cuts off every branch in me that bears no fruit, while every branch that does bear fruit He trims clean so that it will be even more fruitful.'[3]

The reason for this pruning is simple: a vine that is left to itself will produce much wood but little fruit. If the Lord allows us to be at peace for too long, we may easily become tasteless and complacent. Wine likewise tastes best when it is poured from one jar to the other, because the unwanted sediment falls to the bottom before it is discarded.

'Moab has been at rest since youth, like wine left on its dregs, not poured from one jar to another – she has not gone into exile. So she tastes as she did, and her aroma is unchanged.'[4]

We, who are so enamoured with the easy life, rarely appreciate the Lord's designs during these unsettling periods. We feel insecure, resentful even, as He 'empties us from vessel to vessel.' Of this we can be certain: the Lord would not be putting us through such experiences unless He knew they were necessary, both in order to fashion His purposes for us, and His life within us.

'He must become greater . . .'

Elijah has often been compared with John the Baptist. Both were the foremost preachers of their day, as well as the moral conscience of the nation. John had been recognised from before his birth as a chosen man of God, but the day came when one greater than himself was found preaching on his patch. Did he feel resentful or jealous because his ministry was being superseded? Not in the slightest. John recognised in this man the Messiah he himself had foretold, and his unspeakably humble words echo down to us through the centuries.

> *'He must increase* (become greater) *but I must decrease* (become less).'[5]

Perhaps in no other gesture can John's greatness be so clearly seen than in his willingness to hand his own followers over to Jesus. John's attitude is the perfect antidote to all forms of jealousy, and a poignant reminder that we are to gear all our spiritual work, not to fulfilling ourselves, but to preparing the Bride for the Bridegroom.[6]

The most moving story I have heard along these lines again concerns F.B. Meyer. The time came when this anointed minister was superseded in popularity as a conference speaker by a younger man, one Campbell Morgan. For a time Meyer had to wrestle with the understandable pain of seeing his followers turning elsewhere for their spiritual nourishment. Then he hit upon a splendid way of overcoming his disappointment. He resolved to spend as much of his spare time as he could praying for the success of Campbell's ministry. Would that all ministers of the gospel were prepared to do the same!

The Hidden Sacrifice

Understanding little, but doubtless wondering much, Elijah set out for Zarephath, embracing a summons that must have seemed like a contradiction to his life-calling. Submission means placing our future in the Lord's hands, and willingly allowing Him to choose where we should go, and even the means by which He will provide for us. We dare not boast, 'Tomorrow I will do this or that.' It is the direct command of Scripture that we should say, 'If the Lord wills, we will live and do this or that.' Even the Lord Jesus was heard 'because of His reverent submission.'[7]

At the heart of most anointed ministries we will find acts of hidden obedience. When Abraham was called to sacrifice his son, he did not argue with the Lord, but simply told his servants that he intended to go to Mount Moriah and worship. This, the first time the word 'worship' appears in Scripture, shows that the whole concept of worship is undergirded by sacrifice, right from the beginning. A better understanding of this would go a long way to counteract the brasher elements that have become so widespread in certain parts of the Church.

In many ways, Abraham's three-day march to sacrifice his son prefigures the terrible moment when the Father watched and waited as His own Son walked out to die. Abraham appears never to have doubted that God still intended to fulfil His earlier promise, even though He was taking away the son through whom the promise had been destined to come.

God was pleased with Abraham's uncomplaining obedience.[8] At the very last moment a voice came from heaven to bid him stay his hand, and Isaac's life was gloriously spared. It was Abraham's heart God had wanted all along – not Isaac's life. The provision of a ram, as an alternative sacrifice, is testimony to the truth that, even in the midst of our strangest testings, we will find God tender beyond our wildest imaginings – and abundantly able to lead us along His chosen path.

Reflections

Much the Lord does in our lives appears bewildering at the time. Later, we may be better placed to appreciate the reason for His actions – or, at least, to perceive the grace that was with us during those times of testing. Would we not consider our present uncertainties in a very different light if we could enjoy by faith the understanding that hindsight alone usually brings?

Think of examples of 'strange guidance' in your own life. What have you learnt from them?

Selah

Lord Jesus, grant me the grace to yield to You, and to trust You, even when I cannot understand what You are doing. Grant me, too, the faith to affirm and build up others during their dark times. In Jesus' name, Amen.

References

1. Since the Lord often seems to lead us in ways which appear strange to the outsider, we are wise if we leave the matter of our reputation firmly in the Lord's hands – especially if we are leaders! (See John 5:44)
2. The fact that the Lord Jesus received much of His support from women was a revolutionary concept for His day (Luke 8:3)
3. John 15:1–2; cf Hebrews 12:5–11
4. Jeremiah 48:11, cf Deuteronomy 32:11
5. John 3:27–30
6. John 3:29
7. James 4:13–17; Hebrews 5:7
8. Genesis 22:3–5, 15–18; cf Romans 4:11

Chapter 6

The Provision of the Lord

'I have commanded a widow in that place to supply you with food.' (1 Kings 17:9)

In a way, it must have been hard for Elijah to say goodbye to the familiar wadi of Cherith. It hurts when we have to leave places which have meant a lot to us, and where we have met the Lord – but when He shows us that the time has come to move on, we must not hold back. We are a pilgrim people.

Nevertheless, we can imagine all sorts of conflicting thoughts racing through Elijah's mind as he trudged across the wilderness. 'A widow woman. How on earth will I recognise her? How can she provide for me?' Tired and thirsty, it would have been understandable if Elijah allowed his mind to daydream as he drew near to Zarephath. Perhaps God had some well-to-do widow living in a palatial inheritance waiting to take care of him! The reality was far different. As he reached the entrance to the town, he met a widow in the last throes of starvation, forlornly preparing what she fully expected to be her last meal on earth.

We can easily picture this scene. I saw a strikingly similar episode recently on television. An aged Albanian widow had gathered a few twigs together in a last desperate attempt to keep warm. She too had no food left to eat, and was gathering together the little she had before settling down to die. That is the reality of famine, now as then.

Few issues test our relationship with God more sharply than material hardships. By making His servant dependent for his lodging on a widow, the Lord was insisting once again that Elijah did not look to any earthly source to meet his needs. I sometimes think that the Lord specialises in providing for us through means we would not have chosen for ourselves.

Let's face it. Many of us only really begin to realise how wonderfully the Lord has provided for us when He appears to withhold His supplies of blessing. Human nature being what it is, we take miracles that are endlessly repeated for granted. It was not long before the Israelites forgot the heavenly origin of their daily manna, and started to complain that their diet was monotonous.

When something that means a great deal to us is taken away, there are strong temptations to think resentful thoughts towards God. We may even begin to wonder if what we had formerly considered to have been the Lord's miraculous provision was not, in reality, merely something we had contrived by our own efforts.

What happens to us may not be according to our wishes, but that is not to say that it is contrary to His will. The Lord's deliverance comes neither too quickly nor too late. His timing is as exquisite as the means of accomplishing His purposes are unforeseeable. His provision, if not always abundant, will at least always be sufficient. Moreover, it comes from one day to the next, as and when it is needed. We cannot receive grace today to meet tomorrow's needs.

Buoyed up by the recollection of how God had sent him 'meals on ravens' for as long as he had needed them, and heartened that the Lord had fulfilled the first part of His word by leading him to a widow, Elijah's faith rose to the challenge. He trusted that the Lord must be able to provide for them both. After all, God promises to make a way forward in every test and difficulty that we face.[1]

> *'Elijah said to her, "Don't be afraid. Go home and do as you have said. But first make a small cake of bread for me from what you have and bring it to me, and then make something for yourself and your son. For this is what the Lord, the God of Israel says: 'The jar of flour will not be used up, and the jug of oil will not run dry until the day the Lord gives rain on the land.'"'*[2]

What courage it takes to speak with faith and authority in the face of such a desperate situation! Had the Lord not confirmed the word Elijah had spoken so boldly, this would have been their first and last meal together on earth.

Before God performed a miracle of provision, however, He first accomplished a near miracle in human relationships. Just as Elijah had obeyed an improbable word in coming to Zarephath in the first place, so now the Lord turned the heart of this woman to obey His servant. Like the widow who put her all into the Temple Treasury, here was a woman who was willing to share all she had to live on, and that with a complete stranger. She too would have her reward. Because she did as Elijah had told her, there was food every day for Elijah, and for the woman and her family too.

> *'For the jar of flour was not used up and the jug of oil did not run dry, in keeping with the word of the Lord spoken by Elijah.'*[2]

The Generosity of God

In these days, when financial pressures are assailing so many, it is good to ponder the implications of this miracle. Though we cannot always see how it is possible, God will continue to take care of all our needs, material as well as spiritual. All the Accuser's 'prophecies' of impending doom will be shown to be ill-founded as we meet our needs head-on with faith in the Living God, as Elijah did.

How generous the Lord is to those whose hearts are generous![3] When the angel appeared to Cornelius, his first words to him revealed that his almsgiving, as well as his prayers, had ascended as a memorial before God.[4] Nothing we do passes unseen in the courts of Heaven. He takes note not only of what we give, but also of the spirit in which we give it.

The Lord of Hosts provides for His people! A modern-day 'jug of oil' story comes from God's miraculous provision during the horrors of the Second World War. Imprisoned for protecting Jews, Corrie Ten Boom relates how a bottle of essential vitamins renewed itself for weeks on end, for the benefit of the inmates of Ravensbruck concentration camp.

Corrie herself was continually amazed at the kindness and hospitality she received after her miraculous release from Ravensbruck. She asked the Lord one day why people were always so kind to her. He replied that it was because her mother had kept an open kitchen during the years of the Depression. Corrie 'inherited' the blessings her mother had sown.

As Matthew Henry so aptly put it, 'He who ordains the voyage, victuals the ship accordingly.' The miracle of the flour and the oil that were continually renewed, like the loaves and the fishes, is a reminder that God takes the little we offer Him, and gives it power to expand beyond what is humanly possible. Once we have taken all the steps we can in a situation, it is our Lord's joy, as well as His responsibility, to provide for His people.[5]

A Heart to Give

The love of God is nothing if not practical. As we have been provided for, so we can seek to provide for others. Blessing comes ultimately not to those who hoard, but to those who are willing to give of what they have received – their time and talents as well as their material wealth.[6]

As the days get darker, it is increasingly important for Christians to be on the alert to look after one another.[7] Some may be too proud, and some too shy to ask for help, but we must stay alert to people's needs and take appropriate action.

Given the sheer number of needs we encounter, we will benefit by treating the subject of our giving both prayerfully and imaginatively. I was much impressed by the example of David Wilkerson, who used to pray with his wife at the start of each month as to where the Lord would have them send money from a special 'burden' fund they set up in addition to their regular giving.

How true Jesus' words are, that where our treasure is, there too our heart will be. Like the Macedonian churches, we must give to the point where we are giving of the substance as well as the overflow of our lives. If our giving is costing us something, we will be far less likely to develop a superior or a condescending attitude.

The Elijah heart stands at complete variance with the modern tendency to want to have it all. Donald Olsen summed up the absurdity of this spirit thus:

> 'Mr average North American is the instalment buyer who is busy buying things he does not want, with money he does not have, in order to impress people he does not like!'

Remembering Jesus' warning that we cannot serve both God and Mammon, it is good to remind ourselves that it is better to love people and to use things, than to love things and to use people.

Whoever sows generously will also reap generously. Let

us be eager, therefore, to provide for ourselves treasure in heaven. This does not mean that we are never to indulge ourselves in the occasional treat; it is simply an invitation to godly and responsible stewardship in our whole approach to handling worldly wealth.

For myself, I would rather support causes which non-Christians would not readily subscribe to: labourers in the vineyard, rather than the fabric of old buildings. To do this effectively, we should strive to live somewhat below the level of our income, so that the Lord can use the surplus to support others. Life being what it is, this may well prove impossible, but it is, at least, a worthy aim. After all, is it fair to pray for Christian work to be supported, if we ourselves are not prepared to do much about it?

Reflections

The God of Elijah is still at work to this day to provide for the needs of His people. Look back and recall some of the ways in which God has provided for you over the years. Record occasions when you have been as fearfully unbelieving as the Israelites, only to be surprised by joy as the Lord has opened up some new (and usually unexpected) means of provision at just the right time.

Dare to thank and praise the Lord that He will continue to supply your daily bread, along with everything else that you truly need. Then ask Him to show you if there is anything you are spending money on that is not in line with His wishes. Ask Him, too, whether there is any person, cause or organisation that He would have you give to, or contribute more to.

> *'Over and above all this that I have provided, I have given silver and gold from my personal property because of my love for God's Temple. Now who else is willing to give a generous offering to the Lord?'*[8]

Selah

Thank You, Lord, for the way You draw people to share in Your work of provision. You saw the spirit in which the widow shared her livelihood with Elijah, just as You watched another widow put her all into the Temple Treasury. Thank You that the gifts and resources of Your people can help Your Kingdom to spread. I ask that I may play my part in this holy work. May the motivation of my heart, and the gift of my hand alike be pleasing in Your sight. In Jesus' name, Amen.

References

1. 1 Corinthians 10:13
2. 1 Kings 17:13–16; cf Isaiah 46:3–4
3. Proverbs 22:9
4. Acts 10:4
5. Some biblical references to God providing for His people in time of famine include: Deuteronomy 2:7; 1 Kings 17:6, 16; 2 Kings 3:20, 4:6, 7:8; Matthew 14:20.

   The following texts will help us to enter more fully into this subject of seeing God as our Provider: 2 Corinthians 9:6–15; Psalms 65:9, 104:27–29, 132:15ff; Isaiah 55:10; Romans 8:32; Psalm 84:11.
6. Matthew Henry wrote, 'When we can cheerfully provide for others, out of our own necessary provision, as the widow of Zarephath did for Elijah, and Christ for His five thousand guests, and trust God to provide for us by some other way, this is thank-worthy' (cf 2 Corinthians 8).
7. cf Leviticus 25:35:

   'If one of your countrymen becomes poor and is unable to support himself among you, help him as you would an alien or a temporary resident, so that he can continue to live among you.'
8. 1 Chronicles 29:3, 5, 9, 12–14; see also Psalm 128:2; Luke 12:33; Matthew 6:24; Job 31:24–28; Nehemiah 9:20–21

Chapter 7

In the Power of the Spirit

> *'Some time later the son of the woman who owned the house became ill. He grew worse and worse, and finally stopped breathing. She said to Elijah, "What do you have against me, man of God? Did you come to remind me of my sin and kill my son?"'* (1 Kings 17:17–18)

In the power of the Spirit, Elijah had predicted the impossible: that the jar of flour and the jug of oil would not run out. The Lord had worked a miracle, and now, in gratitude, the widow invited the prophet to come and live in the house she shared with her son. Thus Elijah entered into a relatively settled existence for the next three years – a far longer 'sabbatical' than most Christian workers will ever enjoy.

It says much for Elijah's character that he was able to adjust to a life of quiet domesticity. There are some who can prosper in the silence and solitude of Cherith, but who find the rigours and demands of home life irksome. Impatient and intolerant responses reveal how wide is the gap between high-faluting professions of faith and the true condition of their heart.

There are many who like nothing better than to be in the midst of the action. They thrive on the challenge of 'Mount

Carmel-style' confrontations and 'power encounters'. In the process, however, they become addicted to the glamour and excitement of high-powered ministry, and find little to satisfy their restless spirits in the regular round of everyday life.

Whether we like it or not, constant change is here to stay. Much though we would love good times to last forever, it cannot be. Friends move on, we are obliged to change jobs, our pastor leaves, and things can never be quite the same as they were before. May the Lord give us grace and flexibility to adapt to new circumstances!

The Power of Gentleness

There are few things harder to bear than seeing hopes that had been raised being dashed. Before the miracle that had multiplied the oil and the flour, the widow had resigned herself to die. Now, having come to expect a full life-span for herself and her son, her peaceful existence was shattered in the space of a few cruel hours by the tragedy of her only son falling ill and dying. She had poured herself into the boy, and her will to live collapsed. Forgetting all the blessing he had brought, she rounded on Elijah, and accused the prophet who had decreed the famine, of being the cause of this tragedy too.

Only those who have experienced the death of a child in the family can fully understand the devastating intensity of her feelings. But Elijah must have felt the loss almost as keenly. Quite apart from his natural grief, the death of the widow's son posed him an acute threat. Had Satan struck the boy to have him driven out of the home? Where would he go if she threw him out of her house?

Even when the roof over our head is not riding on an issue, it is never easy to be blamed unjustly. To be the target of someone else's anger exposes our own insecurities. Knowing these things makes us admire Elijah's response the more. If he had replied to the distraught woman in anger, he would have fallen into the devil's trap, and would have missed a unique opportunity to experience the power of the Lord. In this moment of extreme crisis, the prophet displayed not only outstanding faith, but also a graciousness which is the hallmark of intimacy with God.

This is, unfortunately, not always true of those who move in prophetic dimensions. Bearing in mind that we pass on to others what we are, rather than merely what we say, we should seek the fruit of gentleness in our lives. Gentleness is used in Scripture in contrast to contentiousness; it by no means implies weakness or woolliness.

When leaders are truly gentle in spirit, then the chances are that their flock will also become mature and settled. Gentleness is the very opposite of that stentorian dragooning and haranguing to which so many leaders subject their precious troops.[1] Gentleness makes us winsome in the sight of God and man.

The Power of the Lord

Elijah could make no more sense of the tragedy than the widow, but when the test came, his faith rose to the occasion. In Elijah's hour of need we see the fruit of his intimacy with the Lord: a wholehearted identification and a genuine compassion. Here are costly qualities we would do well to emulate. The word for 'compassion' in Greek, might loosely be translated as a 'gut ache'. Whenever it is recorded that the Lord Jesus felt compassion, we see the power of God flowing most freely through Him to heal. Scripture urges us towards such whole-hearted participation in each other's sufferings.[2]

We have no way of knowing for certain, but the wording of the widow's outburst makes one suspect that there may have been some guilt attached to the birth of the boy. If this is so, we can imagine how easily she would have been inclined to view her son's death as a direct punishment from God. It certainly shattered her faith.

Elijah had to overcome not only the widow's anger, but also the repugnance any Jew would have felt at having to touch a corpse. Taking her son in his arms, he carried him to the upper room and laid him on his bed. Then, stretching himself out on top of the boy's body, he cried out to God from the depths of his heart:

> *'O Lord my God, have You brought tragedy also upon this widow I am staying with, by causing her son to die? O Lord my God, let this boy's life return to him!'*[3]

We can feel the intensity of this prayer. Perhaps Elijah himself was feeling distressed and angry that the Lord had allowed this situation to come about. What a blaze of joy he must have felt as the child began to breathe again![4] How moving that it should be here, far from the Promised Land, that we come across the first recorded instance in Scripture of someone being raised from the dead.

We can imagine the reunion, as he took the child downstairs and presented him alive to his mother. The Lord had restored not only the widow's son, but her own heart too. From that moment on she would have been able to enjoy much closer fellowship with Elijah; now, at last, she trusted him. More importantly, she trusted his God. Where, before, she may have been little more than a nominal believer, now her heart was convinced.

> *'Then the woman said to Elijah, "Now I know that you are a man of God, and that the word of the Lord from your mouth is the truth."'*[5]

Elijah spent the next few years with the widow in Zarephath; a pleasant town, with the steep snow-clad slopes of Mount Hermon behind him, and fine views over the blue

Mediterranean. After the agony of watching first the shrinking brook and then the dying boy, Elijah was rewarded with a long stretch of calm: quite possibly, the most settled period of his whole life. Such interludes are to be savoured to the full.

Authority in Prayer

It is intriguing to note how many of the prayers Jesus and His disciples prayed took the form of commands. When faced by a sudden storm, the Lord Jesus did not ask His Father for rescue: He commanded the storm to be still. When He found Simon's mother-in-law in bed with a fever He did not send for a thermometer: He rebuked the fever. The apostles prayed along similar lines.[6]

Smith Wigglesworth, an early Pentecostal leader, declared that 'an ounce of faith is worth a ton of asking,' because he rightly saw that so much of our prayer is little more than the vocalising of our unbelief. It certainly falls well short of the confident petition Paul had in mind when he told us that in everything by prayer and supplication, with thanksgiving, we should let our requests be made known to God.[7]

We need to make our faith comprehensive, to encompass every part of our lives. The prayer of faith mentioned in James 5:15 is both specific and definite. It enables us to exercise the authority of the Lord over Satan, sickness, and other difficult situations. This is less a matter of finding the right words – let alone a formula – than the Holy Spirit within us conferring the authority and anointing to pray in a particular way.

It is hardly to be wondered at that Satan endeavours so strenuously to keep believers from using the authority that is ours in the name of the Lord Jesus. The powers of darkness know only too well that such faith can release the power of the Lord in a way in which months of merely praying about a situation may not succeed in doing. There comes a moment to stop circling the walls of Jericho, and to utter the shout which brings them down. Such was the faith Elijah exercised when he cried out for life to return to the widow's son.

At the end of that momentous day, Elijah and the widow could agree together:

> *'God is our refuge, and our strength, an ever present help in trouble. Therefore we will not fear.'*[8]

The Battle for the Next Generation

Elijah's struggle to save a child from premature death points us to the intense spiritual battle we are waging today for the next generation. Has there ever been a time before when we have had to pray so hard for protection against the effects of secular and sinister influences in the lives of our children? Worldly stereotypes that embrace amoral and positively anti-Christian values confront our children daily in society and in our schools.[9]

A stable family is a powerful demonstration of the reality of God's love. The fact that there are so few of them about is a measure of the enemy's hostility. Most of us go out from home to work and do battle for the Lord. By the time we return home, our thoughts are often centred on the need to rest and recuperate. We are glad to relax, but we often let our defences down too far, and end up hurting those closest to us by our harsh words and thoughtless actions. How important it is to deal promptly with little seeds of resentment and frustration before they develop into suffocating weeds of indifference or intolerance.

The extent to which Christian marriage is under threat today would have been unthinkable a generation or two ago. Yet the problems we experience would be greatly reduced if we would admit our difficulties and temptations and pray for each other more honestly.

Like vintage wines, Christian marriages should improve as the years pass by. It is just as important in marriage to try to be the right sort of person as it was to meet the right partner in the first place. Many of us husbands need to be more imaginative in expressing our love for our wives – just as some women would do well to show that they love their husbands as well as the Lord. Intimacy with God means being at one with our loved ones too.

Because the pressures on family life are so great, it pays to make the effort to get away together before crises develop. The strains that ensue from not doing so may not be apparent at the time, but are cumulative, manifesting themselves at times of heightened tension, or when the children have finally flown the nest.

Times away are an excellent opportunity to restore both personal intimacy and the habit of praying together. But since the Lord bestows countless answers through those who pray together, we can be sure the enemy will do all he can to deter our life of prayer together. Heart-unity is our vital responsibility, so that nothing will hinder our prayers.[10]

The fact that Elijah was called to lodge with a widow, however, speaks directly to God's concern for the many single parents of our own day. The Lord does not discard the disadvantaged; rather, He sovereignly chooses them to further the purposes of His Kingdom.

Reflections

How we respond in the face of tragedy depends, to a large extent, on how far we have allowed the power of the Lord to touch our heart. Like Elijah, we too will find ourselves subjected to serious tests of faith. The way Elijah handled his sudden crisis is an inspiration to us in at least five ways:

1. Crises in the Family

Perhaps, like the widow, you too, are in need of a miracle of grace for a member of your family. You have prayed and prayed, but nothing appears to have changed. Further discernment may be needed, especially for generational problems, but do not give up praying now. The Lord hears the cry of your heart. You may be well-advised, however, to ask friends who are less emotionally involved to help you carry the weight of the burden. They can often see issues more clearly, and can release the spiritual authority of objective faith into situations which are weighing you down.[11]

2. The Power of Rounding up Prayer

The more we are seeking to lead an Elijah-style life of truly seeking after God, the more confidently we can expect miraculous answers to prayer. At times of urgent need, however, we need people who will pray with and for us.

I cannot stress too much how important it is to establish lines of communication in prayer before we need to use them. Then, when a crisis develops, we are able to harness prayer straight away. Examine your own 'lines of communication'. Is there anything you can do to improve them?

3. Growth in Character

Elijah's faith-filled response to the tragedy enabled the widow to 'catch' his faith. Words are powerful (especially when there is a holy man or woman behind them) but it is ultimately who we are, and what we do, that is the yardstick of our intimacy with God.

To illustrate how important this dimension of our character is, may I invite you to close your eyes and think back to one or two of your earliest teachers. Bless their memory as they come to mind.

Of all the thousands of words these people must have addressed to you, how many can you remember now? Is it not rather the impression of the person that is stamped in the memory banks of your mind? For better or for worse these people helped to shape your life.

Pray to be a man or woman who can respond to crises with faith, and whose character shows forth the likeness of our Risen Saviour.

4. The Witness of the Church

We can imagine that this miracle made a profound impact on the boy himself as he grew up. Remembering that more than 75% of all conversions happen before a person reaches the age of twenty one, pray for the Church's efforts to reach a generation that is growing up with so little knowledge of God.

5. The Value of Fellowship

It is impossible to overstate how precious fellowship with the renewed widow would have been for Elijah. Exiled by the Lord in a foreign land, where he had no fellow believers with whom to share his faith, their relationship reminds us that we should never underestimate the blessing our letters and phone calls can be to those who find themselves far from home. Is there anyone the Lord would have you get in contact with now?

Selah

> Lord Jesus, help us to move in the power of your Spirit. Grant us faith for every situation that comes our way, and a character that speaks of You. We cry out to You for protection against all the destructive forces that assail our generation. We pray particularly for families to grow in the grace of the Lord; for the love of husbands and wives to deepen with the passing of

the years, and for our children to be true to You. May the fruit of gentleness be seen in Your Church, so that many may come to know the grace of God for themselves. In Jesus' name, Amen.

References

1. I would commend *Understanding Leadership*, by Tom Marshall (Sovereign World) as being the finest book on leadership I have read.
2. Matthew 9:36, 14:14, 15:32, 18:27, 20:34; Mark 1:41, 6:34, 8:2; Luke 7:13
3. 1 Kings 17:20–21
4. 1 Kings 17:22
5. 1 Kings 17:19–24
6. e.g. Matthew 8:26; Luke 4:38–39; Acts 3:1–8; cf Acts 14:10; Revelation 2:26–27
7. Philippians 4:6
8. Psalm 46:1–2
9. Nowhere is this more clearly seen than in most people's attitude towards abortion.
10. 1 Peter 3:7
11. This episode hints at the different realms of public and private prayer. Elijah did not pray for the boy in the widow's presence, because he needed time to wait on the Lord privately. Public prayer requires shared discernment amongst believers as to what it is we should be praying for. Private prayer is when we cry out to the Lord concerning issues that burden us individually. In both cases this seeking of the Lord's heart and will enables things to come about which would not otherwise have happened.

Chapter 8

The Stature of Waiting

'After a long time, in the third year, the word of the Lord came to Elijah, "Go and present yourself to Ahab, and I will send rain on the land." So Elijah went to present himself to Ahab.' (1 Kings 18:1)

Put yourself in Elijah's shoes and try to imagine how he felt during those long years at Zarephath. With no official role to play, or any function to fulfil, it would have been easy for him to have begun to wonder if God Himself had not passed him by. After all, he was still no nearer to fulfilling his goal than he had been on that distant day, three and more years before, when he had delivered his original word and been forced to flee from Ahab's wrath.

It is hard for those of us who live in well-watered lands to imagine the desolation three years of drought would have caused. Life must have come to a virtual standstill throughout the nation because, unlike Egypt which could be irrigated from the Nile, God had designed Israel to be dependent on regular rainfall. He had also warned that this would be withheld if the nation backslid![1]

God had promised that He would end the drought through Elijah's mouth. How often the prophet must have wondered during the next few years whether the time had come for him to go back home and release the rains.

Elijah's heart must have leapt when he heard the Lord promising to send rain again. It was not that the nation had truly repented of its evil, but rather that He had heard the prayers of His intercessor and was prepared to show His mercy. Accompanying the promise, however, was a specific condition: God would send rain on the land again only if Elijah was prepared to risk another visit to the king who had vowed to kill him!

I have the feeling that many of us who claim to trust in the Lord are secretly quite happy to rely most of the time on our own resources. But God sometimes makes that option impossible for us. Faith has always to be tested.[2]

Elijah's prolonged stay in Zarephath is a reminder that we need patience, as well as zeal, to fulfil the will of the Lord. Before we set off with Elijah on his all-important journey to meet Ahab, we will do well to consider in more detail why the Lord obliged him to spend so much of his time waiting.

Life itself is, in one sense, a period of waiting, and of preparation for eternity. This may be hard for some of us to grasp, because our perception of waiting typically centres around specific dates and desires, in which case all we are really interested in is the arrival of the event – be it a birthday, a promotion, a holiday, or a deliverance from some difficulty or danger.

The Hebrew concept of waiting is far richer, in that it embraces the connotation of entwining ourselves in God. Rather than viewing times of waiting (with all their attendant uncertainty) as being merely something to be endured, we will fare better if we can learn to discern a purpose and a stature that elevate them into an authentic part of our pilgrimage.

Some years ago I came across a book called *The Stature of Waiting* by W.H. Vanstone.[3] Vanstone challenges, in a variety of ways, the idea that a man's dignity consists solely in his outward achievements. Central to his argument is his illustration of the way in which our Lord's ministry changed from being an active one to a passive one.

Throughout the greater part of the gospel narrative we see the Lord Jesus initiating and directing events. The verbs associated with His ministry tend therefore to be 'active' ones. Jesus healed, He preached, He cast out demons, He walked from one village to another, He encouraged, He rebuked and so on. He had warned His disciples, however, that the 'day' during which He could work would be of limited duration.[4] The night of darkness He had spoken of began when Judas made his fateful decision to betray His master.

This action heralds a change in the focus of the gospels, a shift that is mirrored by the verbs used to describe our Lord's ministry. In the portion of the Gospels which we call the Passion, the key verbs revert to the passive voice. Working gives way to waiting as the most appalling injustices and atrocities are inflicted on the Lord Jesus. He was betrayed, arrested, interrogated, persecuted, sentenced by a prejudiced court, brutally flogged and finally crucified.

In John 17:4 Jesus declared that He had completed the work that His Father had sent Him to do. In John 19:28, however, He perceived that all things were now completed. Since His work had already been completed, something more than 'work' was therefore needed to save mankind: namely His own suffering and sacrifice.

The Lord Jesus had declared in John 10:17–18 that the reason the Father loved Him was because He intended to lay down His life. Without this sacrifice His mission would have been incomplete. Whereas His active ministry reached only a comparatively limited number of people, now, by His Passion on the Cross, the barrier between God and man was taken away once and for all.

Beyond our Control

How incredible it is that the salvation of the world should hinge on the Lord Jesus 'handing Himself over' to be crucified. It is an unexpected, and an undramatic way to describe so mighty an event.[5] Jesus not only 'handed over' His active ministry, He also laid down something infinitely more precious: His perfect and unbroken relationship with His Father, as He became a once-for-all offering for sin.

It is obvious that our Lord's sufferings are on an altogether different scale from our own trials and tribulations, but there are enough overlaps with our own experience to make it relevant to our condition. When Jesus was handed over to be crucified, He experienced something that is ultimately common to all people, namely, that of being (humanly speaking) no longer in control of His circumstances.

We, too, share in His passion in that we are sometimes called to wait rather than to work. Whether it takes the form of unemployment, hospitalisation, bereavement or some other major upheaval, events occur to and around us which we would not have chosen for ourselves. There are few things most of us find more disorientating.

If we are to attain to a stature of waiting, rather than experiencing constant anxiety on account of the uncertainties that we face, the most precious thing we can give to God is our active trust that He is still in control. The more surrendered we are, the more the Lord is able to use these things for His glory.

Times and Seasons

The kingdom of God does not advance by reacting passively to circumstances, but through determined prayer and decisive action. If the devil can make us lethargic and passive, we are well on our way to being defeated. Yet all of us will experience occasions when we have no option but to wait for an illness to pass, or for a 'dark night of the soul' to dissolve into the warmth of His presence.

The fact that Lord Jesus was following a heavenly-decreed timetable is important. Notwithstanding the wonderful prophecies that had been given at the time of His birth, the Lord Jesus worked and waited as a carpenter until the moment came to show Himself to the nation. There was a time for Him to lead a hidden life, a time to show Himself to the nation – and then, finally, a time to suffer. Jesus' brothers could not grasp this calling, but urged Him to show Himself to the world, and prove that He was someone special.[6] But the Lord steadfastly refused to comply with anyone else's expectations, or to take premature action.

As sailors respect and understand the tides and seasons, so we must seek to be as open as we can be to the timing of the Holy Spirit. If that means waiting patiently while months turn into years, as it did for Elijah in Zarephath, and for Moses during those forty long years in the wilderness, then so be it.

If we can avoid becoming unduly discouraged through adversity, and unwisely exalted through success, then we will have much to offer in the exciting and challenging days that lie ahead. It is those whose hearts have been prepared by years of hidden service who will prove the least vulnerable to pride or deception when the full onslaught of temptation comes their way.

Delays that Glorify God

We may often be tempted to complain at God's delays, but there are good reasons for them. Some of the delays we experience, are of course, the direct result of opposing forces. Just as demonic hindering delayed the answer to Daniel's prayer, so we too will frequently experience the opposition of unseen foes as we wrestle to achieve the will of God.[7] Determined intercession is a proper response when we sense that demonic forces are involved in causing delays. But there are other delays which God uses for His higher purposes. We need discernment when to wrestle, and when to nestle.

How, for example, are we to interpret the Lord Jesus's decision to remain where He was, when He was informed that His good friend Lazarus was seriously ill? Humanly speaking, He stayed until it was too late to be of any help – even though He knew how much distress His failure to come would cause Mary and Martha. He waited, because He knew that there would be more glory through raising Lazarus from the dead, than if He had rushed to heal him.[8]

Only this week I heard a story along similar lines concerning a minister, who had battled in vain to teach his large, but complacent, congregation the ways of God. The Lord allowed him to experience such a serious illness that he was forced to offer his resignation. The same night after this had been announced, the Lord visited him. The minister's health was completely restored, and the Church knew that it had come face to face with a miracle. It made a most profound impact on the congregation.

Beyond the Wilderness

I believe that God takes us into times of wilderness and waiting precisely in order to show us that His eye is constantly on us, even during those times when we are least aware of it. It is not our feelings God requires so much as a response of faith. When we harness our sense of helplessness to the unlimited power of God, we will find that He has been seeking all along the very best way of resolving all our difficulties.

When the Lord leads us along stretches of white water, it

is as well to be aware that we will often be offered an easier route. The question then is whether we will allow ourselves to be distracted from following the Lord's command. Hudson Taylor's deeply-felt conviction that the Lord had called him to China, for example, was imperilled by his love for a woman who was unwilling to make the ultimate sacrifice of going with him on the mission field.

I believe that we can trace the origins of the mighty harvest that China is experiencing today to the fact that Hudson Taylor put his calling above the longing of his heart. Moreover, because he had obeyed God in this crucial matter, the Lord led Hudson to another Christian woman while he was in China. His marriage to Maria is one of the great love stories of the Church.

Before the action comes the waiting; before the deliverance, the death of all human hope. When Pharaoh rejected Moses' advances, and worsened the living conditions of the Hebrews, Moses had to face not only the hostility of Pharaoh, but something that must have caused him a still sharper sense of pain: rejection at the hands of his own people.

This is the moment of greatest testing, when everything inside us longs to retreat from so difficult a calling. In his distress, Moses poured out His heart again to God. Once more the Lord reaffirmed His call on his life. He had said that He would bring his people out of Egypt and He had not rescinded His promise.[9]

There is always a danger that we will strive too hard to fulfil the vision God has given us, instead of waiting to let Him bring it about in His way and in His time. It is sinful to try to take by force what God would give by grace. The troubles multiply when we try to force the outcome prematurely. It is all too easy to end up making an 'Ishmael' out of a genuine promise of God.

Waiting stretches our trust precisely because it does not feel as though the Lord is doing anything. Rees Howells, one of the great men of faith of this century, used to say that when we are in the middle of a test, it feels for all the world as though there is no God at all. We are quite wrong, of course, as we always are when our feelings incline us to assume that God has lost interest in us.

True, not everything will come about all at once, but neither does it all depend on our own efforts. There are matters we must pray for, claim even, and then leave to one side until the Spirit prompts again. God will 'activate' the vision in His own good time. For now, it is more important to keep seeking Him from day to day, than straining towards some mythical moment 'when it will all happen'.

I have often pondered St Paul's stated desire to take the gospel to Spain. He never fulfilled, so far as we know, this particular desire. Instead, arrest, and years of imprisonment in far from salubrious Roman jails were to be his lot. A lesser man might well have succumbed to the shock. After all, had he not set out on a mission for God? Far from bemoaning his fate, Paul seized the opportunity to write letters to the churches he had worked so hard to establish; epistles which now form the backbone of the New Testament.

What a way to redeem a seeming tragedy! If Paul had fulfilled his original desire and ministered to the peoples of Spain, perhaps, at best, a vigorous church might have been established in that one country. As it was, countless millions throughout the world have been strengthened, because Paul overcame his disappointment, put pen to paper, and shared the priceless wisdom the Lord had given him.

If you have grown weary of waiting for the Lord to deliver you from some particular problem, or to fulfil a specific promise, remember how Mary pondered in her heart all that she had seen and heard, but made no attempt to act ahead of the Lord's initiative. If the Lord's leading sometimes seems on the slow side, remember that He is testing and training us for eternity.

Reflections

Does this teaching on there being a 'stature' of waiting make sense of certain delays in your own life? I mentioned at the beginning of this book the value of waiting quietly on the Lord by making good use of the Reflections and Selahs. It may well be that you are beginning to omit some of these exercises in your eagerness to continue reading the text. Perhaps now would be a good time to remind you of my opening comments, and to feast on these still moments of reflection before the Lord.

Suppose you are holding a bath sponge tightly in your hand. No matter how long it is immersed, it is impossible to soak up any substantial amount of water. Most of the water is bound to be squeezed out. So it is when we are attempting to receive from the Lord. If we 'tense' ourselves up, we are not going to be still and open enough for the Lord to fill us with all He wants us to have.

Times of waiting afford us with opportunity to take stock and reflect on our life. Have we perhaps 'stayed put' when the Lord has called us to move on? Or moved on, before the Lord has truly released us to? If we know that we have 'missed the boat', or 'jumped the gun' in the past, all is not lost. The Lord will quite possibly offer us another opportunity. He often works circumstances in such a way as to permit us a virtual re-run of situations we handled badly before. His power and presence will be available to help us fare better the second time round.

Selah

> Lord, how hard I find it to wait! Thank You that Elijah refused to return to Israel until You summoned him. Grant me grace to resist the pressure to run ahead of Your leading – and to feel a failure when things do not work out as I had expected. Help me to live in the

overlap between promise and fulfilment, without fretting for answers You are not yet ready to supply. Let me find fulfilment in doing what You guide my hand to do, from one day to the next. In Jesus' name, Amen.

References

1. Long before Israel entered the Promised Land, the Lord spelt out the calamities that would come upon His people if they chose to turn their backs on Him.

   'Be careful, or you will be enticed to turn away and worship other gods and bow down to them. Then the Lord's anger will burn against you, and He will shut the heavens so that it will not rain and the ground will yield no produce, and you will soon perish from the good land the Lord is giving you.' (Deuteronomy 11:16–17)

2. Scripture affords us numerous examples of God's dramatic sense of timing and occasion. For instance, Ezekiel's wife died on the day Nebuchadnezzar besieged Jerusalem; an earthquake occurred at the very moment the Lord Jesus was put to death (Ezekiel 24:15ff; Matthew 27:51–54). Think of other such examples.
3. I was so impressed by Vanstone's treatment of the subject that I have named this chapter after his book. *The Stature of Waiting* is published by Darton, Longman and Todd.
4. John 9:4
5. The same unusual expression is used in Galatians 2:20 and Romans 8:32, as well as in Matthew 24:9 and 26:2.
6. John 7:3–9
7. Daniel 10:12–14
8. John 11:1–44
9. Exodus 5:22–6:10. The Israelites were too discouraged to believe the Lord, however, until both they, and the Egyptians, had seen the mighty displays of the Lord's power.

Chapter 9

Interfacing with the World

> *'As Obadiah was walking along, Elijah met him. Obadiah recognised him, bowed down to the ground and said, "Is it really you, my lord Elijah?" "Yes," he replied, "Go tell your master, 'Elijah is here.'" ... "Haven't you heard, my lord, what I did while Jezebel was killing the prophets of the Lord? I hid a hundred of the Lord's prophets in two caves, fifty in each, and supplied them with food and water."'* (1 Kings 18:7–8, 13)[1]

Torn between gratitude for the way the Lord had preserved him, and his longing to return to Israel, it must have been hard for Elijah to dwell peacefully in Zarephath, knowing the suffering that was even then befalling his fellow believers in Israel.

Suddenly, Elijah's prolonged retreat in the safe, if cloistered, township of Zarephath came to an end. The time had come for Elijah to move beyond the world of private devotion to a public demonstration of his faith. On his way to confront the tyrant king a second time, Elijah met another servant of the Lord, who was, as we shall see, a most unusual person.

Obadiah: Stool-Pigeon or Faithful Servant?

It is a sign of God's favour that He raises certain of His

servants to key positions. Like Joseph, who rose to prominence in Pharaoh's court, Obadiah was placed in charge of Ahab's palace.[2] Obadiah not only kept his faith in that most alien of environments, but used his position to protect other followers of Yahweh. At the risk of his life, he hid and supplied the prophets of God, while famine and persecution raged in the land.

Our hearts rise as we see Elijah coming across this man, whose very name means 'servant of the Lord'. Have we not longed for him during his lonely life to find a worthy companion? Surely in Obadiah he would find a suitable partner?

Yet there is a strange ambiguity in the way Obadiah responded to meeting Israel's most wanted man. Eager though he may have been to relate what he had done to protect the Lord's prophets, the truth was that Elijah's unexpected reappearance had put him in a predicament. If he reported to Ahab that he had sighted him, might the capricious king not accuse him of having known all along where the prophet had been hiding? And suppose Elijah had disappeared by the time he returned? You can never be too careful with prophets! Before returning to Ahab's presence, Obadiah extracted from Elijah the promise that he would present himself to the king that very day.

The praise and fame that come our way in life test us just as thoroughly as the more distressing situations.[3] Bribed by pleasure, and frightened at the thought of losing face, many who rise to positions of leadership and power soon become preoccupied with their own survival. It is hard not to wonder whether Obadiah had come to look a little too much at his own self-interest. His timidity stands in sharp contrast with Elijah's dauntless courage.[4]

Reaching out to Others

A question we must all face is how we can translate a

devotional life of some beauty and excellence into a telling presence for the Lord. Of the many in the nation who still adhered to the God of Israel, only Elijah had the courage to speak out, and call its leaders to repentance.

As friends of Jesus, we must never lose our concern to introduce people to the Saviour of the World. The Lord has placed each one of us in a unique position to reach out to particular people with the love of God. Our place of work is the most visible demonstration by which people can observe how real God is to us. Most of us, after all, devote more than fifty percent of our waking hours to our jobs, and it is right to pray that our presence there may make some difference. Yet all too many of us tone down our witness to the point where we succeed neither in challenging, nor in converting anyone.

It is easy to justify our compromise. 'It would be foolish to rock the boat,' we argue. 'Nobody accepts the Christian point of view anyway, so why bother speaking out?' Thus institutions, which are already fallen, risk becoming genuine outposts of the devil's empire, as the ways of godlessness go from strength to strength, unchallenged.

Concerning our witness, it is true that character speaks louder than words. Yet few, if any, will take the step of asking the Lord Jesus into their hearts without clear explanation. When I first saw my future wife at work as a nurse, the love and care that shone from her were a delight to witness. Because she did not speak openly about her faith, however, her patients were left with the impression that she was simply an exceptionally lovely person. Quite unintentionally the 'glory' went to her.

It was far from easy for her to be able to find the words with which to express her faith. It took a considerable amount of time and courage before she was able to do so with any degree of confidence. I praise God that she battled to overcome her embarrassment, because she is able now to witness freely about the Lord Jesus. There have even been numerous occasions when she has felt prompted to pray with non-Christians. Many have then been able to experience the reality of God's love for themselves.

May the Lord challenge our complacency, and bring us face to face with people who, like Elijah, walk so closely to the Lord that their purity exposes the hidden motivations of our hearts. Their wisdom and enthusiasm will inspire us to fresh endeavours for the Kingdom, and we will experience the truth of Paul's prayer:

> *'I pray that you may be active in sharing your faith, so that you will have a full understanding of every good thing we have in Christ.'*[5]

Modern-Day Obadiahs

None of us find it easy to work in a society which holds steeply contrasting views to our own. Nevertheless, it has always been God's will to prosper His people, and to win them favour, even in the eyes of those whose guiding principles differ sharply from our own.

By contrast, those who divide life artificially into the spiritual and the secular, are left with a fragmented and splintered world view. There is nothing biblical about the concept of a 'secular' job, for everything becomes sacred when it is offered to God. The more fully we believe this, the more faithfully we will work and pray for the power of God to move in the place of our employment.

Why is it that we only see the photographs of missionaries serving overseas, pinned up at the back of the church? Would it not be a good idea to recognize the value of every member who is seeking to be a witness for the Lord? Rosalind and I love to visit people at their place of work because it helps us to identify more fully with them. Sometimes this leads to them developing a strategy for impacting it more effectively for the Kingdom.

It is not only conventional missionaries who need our prayer support: it is doctors, nurses, teachers, housewives, businessmen – anyone, in short, who has a heart to share the love of Christ with others. Theirs is a mission field which takes them right onto the front line in the battle against secularism.

To pray for our schools, hospitals and workplaces is to invite the Lord to impact the life of communities with His power. Since we can only give ourselves wholeheartedly to a limited number of causes, it is important for us to know which people, professions, regions or nations the Lord would have us be involved with.

The example of Obadiah reminds us of the need to pray for Christians who have acquired high standing in life. All too often, such people either lack vision for what they are doing, or the prayer support which would make their work fruitful. Rather than pressing them to attend more meetings, or to assume greater responsibilities within the Church, it is for us to make the effort to find out more about their activities.

These are the Obadiahs of our own generation, who must serve in the world, yet remain free of its harmful influences. May we pray, serve and support these people, as they take their stand for Jesus, and live out the greater part of their life in a public arena, in the fear of the Lord.[6]

Reflections

It is wonderful how the Lord raises some of His people to prominent positions – but they need our prayers, not least that they may continue to serve the Lord, rather than their own self-interests. Bring a number of modern-day 'Obadiahs' to the Lord now. Perhaps He will give you an ongoing burden for some of them.

Pray for courage to overcome your natural fear of man, and to have many opportunities to tell them of all the Lord means to you. Ask the Lord if there are any specific steps you can take to be more effective in sharing the love of God with those for whom you have a particular burden.

Selah

We ask Your richest blessings, Lord, on those You have raised to prominence; that their hearts be pure, and their fruitfulness be great. Grant us, too, both courage and wisdom, as we reach out to others with Your love. In Jesus' name, Amen.

References

1. It would be helpful to read vs. 3–15 as well.
2. In his epistle to the Philippians, Paul writes of the believers who belong to Caesar's household (Philippians 3:22). There, in the midst of a way of life that was completely opposed to the Christian ideal, God still had His faithful servants. *'When a man's ways are pleasing to the Lord, He makes even his enemies live at peace with him'* (Proverbs 16:7).
3. Proverbs 27:21
4. Nevertheless, it is recorded that Obadiah feared the Lord greatly (1 Kings 18:3 KJV). It is greatly to his credit that he overcame his fears, and became a vital link in the run-up to the mighty conflict on Mount Carmel. What does the fear of the Lord mean? The simplest definition I can give is that it means we love Him so much, and have such a strong desire to please Him, that we literally fear to do anything that will grieve or displease Him; e.g. Psalms 5:7, 19:9, 111:10; Proverbs 8:13, 14:27, 15:16, 19:23, 23:17, 29:25; Isaiah 11:3, 33:6; 2 Corinthians 5:11, 7:1.
5. Philemon 4–6
6. cf Nehemiah 1:3–11; Daniel 9:15–20; Exodus 32:11–14; 33:13–17

Chapter 10

Fire on Mount Carmel

> '*When* [Ahab] *saw Elijah, he said to him, "Is that you, you troubler of Israel?" "I have not made trouble for Israel," Elijah replied. "But you and your father's family have. You have abandoned the Lord's commands and have followed the Baals."'* (1 Kings 18:17–18)

It was always going to be a stormy confrontation. Ahab would have felt more than mildly apprehensive as he set out to meet the man he perceived to be his chief political opponent. The jittery king promptly accused Elijah of being the cause of all the trouble in Israel, but Elijah flung the taunt back in his face. 'You've got it wrong, Ahab. This drought has come upon the nation because you chose to worship the Baals. You're the real cause of all the trouble – not me!'

The king was dumbfounded. Nobody had ever had the nerve to speak to him like this. The prophet's bravery struck him as forcibly as the truth he was speaking. Unable to deny the accusations, he agreed to the terms of the challenge Elijah proposed: an unprecedented contest which would demonstrate to the nation whether God or Baal was really Lord.[1]

Why did Ahab agree to meet Elijah face to face when he could have sent a patrol to arrest him? The answer is that when we obey what God has shown us to do, it is His joy to bring about the humanly impossible. Moreover, after three years of devastating drought, Ahab could hardly fail to realise the power of God's word through Elijah. What he wanted to know now was whether Elijah really did have the power to make it rain again.

As word of the forthcoming contest was sent out, the people streamed westwards to join the 450 prophets of Baal on Mount Carmel. Prophets require a forum for their message, and Elijah knew that there would never be a better moment to call the nation back to God. At the top of his voice, he presented the people with the clearest challenge they had faced since the days of Joshua.[2]

> 'Why do you labour for food that spoils and that does not endure to eternal life? If the Lord really is the supreme God, then why is He not also your supreme love? *"How long will you waver between two opinions? If the Lord is God, follow Him, but if Baal is God, follow Him."* But the people said nothing.'[3]

When Elijah had finished cutting through their excuses, he knew that something more than words was necessary to rouse the people from their spiritual sloth. Every preacher knows this feeling. The whole galaxy of our modern-day 'gods', with their prized scientific achievements and abundant material possessions, has taken much the same toll on the soul of the nation as the idolatrous Baals did: deadening people to the call of God on our lives.

It is altogether right and proper that we should cry out for a double portion of His Spirit in our own generation, and a renewed demonstration of the power of God.

> *'Then Elijah said to them, "I am the only one of the Lord's prophets left, but Baal has 450 prophets. Get two*

> *bulls for us . . . The god who answers by fire – he is God." Then all the people said, "What you say is good." '*[4]

Elijah summoned his adversaries to prepare a bull and to call down fire from heaven. Like Abraham, who was content to offer Lot the best of the land, he was happy to let his opponents go first in the contest. Both men showed complete confidence that God was bigger than all the odds stacked against them. Elijah rejoiced that he had trapped the prophets of Baal into attempting something he knew to be beyond their powers to perform.[5]

The Longest Day

This whole episode on Mount Carmel is a stunning reminder of what can be achieved by faith in the face of overwhelming odds. Because we know the outcome, we should not be tempted to dismiss the contest as a foregone conclusion. Although the words 'fire' and 'God' are frequently linked in Scripture, the devil, too, has the power to send down fire from heaven.[6] But God would not suffer the devil to intervene, for this was His hour of judgement on the powers of darkness.

For six long hours Elijah endured the rabid sounds of the prophets chanting and shouting to their horrible god. The tension and oppression must have been well nigh overwhelming. Whichever way he looked, he would have seen no friendly face to encourage him.

The devil loves to make us imagine that he is in control of our circumstances. He hates it when we have the courage not to take him seriously![7] The louder his opponents shouted, and the deeper they lacerated themselves in their desperate attempts to release the power of Baal, the bolder Elijah became, taunting them fearlessly.

Now, the moment of reckoning had come. The followers of Baal had to face the fact that their pleas had remained unanswered. All they could hope for was that Elijah's God would prove to be equally as impotent.

In a sense, Elijah's years of being hidden had been but a preparation for this moment. Long before fire fell from heaven and incinerated the sacrifice, his heart had been burning that God should intervene, so that the nation would again worship their God. For that reason alone he was willing to step forward, and cry out for God to demonstrate His power.

Elijah's first action was to take twelve stones, one for each of the tribes, and build an altar to the Lord. This was a symbolic restoration of the altars that Ahab and Jezebel had overthrown. Although only ten tribes were represented on Mount Carmel, Israel had always been one in God's eyes. Elijah offered his sacrifice on behalf of the whole nation.

Then, to prove beyond doubt that nothing is too hard for the God of Israel, Elijah poured twelve full barrels of precious water over the sacrifice. Then he prayed:

> *'"O Lord, God of Abraham, Isaac and Israel, let it be known this day that You are God in Israel, and that I am Your servant and have done all these things at Your command. Answer me, O Lord, answer me, so these people will know that You, O Lord, are turning their hearts back again." Then the fire of the Lord fell and burned up the sacrifice, the wood, the stones and the soil, and also licked up the water in the trench.'*[8]

Whatever the fire might do to the worshippers of Baal, Elijah had no fear that it would hurt him. In a moment of holy terror, Elijah's sacrifice was consumed. What was so extraordinary about this fire is that it blazed from above, rather than from below, as ordinary ones do. It truly was a fire from heaven.[9]

Stunned by what they had witnessed, the people threw

themselves prostrate. Slowly they recovered from their shock and took up a chant. Its echoes rolled around the hillside as they cried aloud, *'The Lord, He is God. The Lord, He is God.'* At last they were willing to commit themselves to the true and living God.

A stand for God means taking a stand against the counterfeit. Judgement was immediately executed on the false prophets. We are spared the gruesome details, being told only that the prophets of Baal were put to the sword in the Kishon valley. A new day had dawned for the people of Israel.

Lessons from Mount Carmel

We can learn important lessons from this amazing episode. Firstly, that it is prayer which releases the power of God – but also that we must take our stand and play our part. Just as Elijah wasted no time in putting to death those who had been robbing the nation of its vitality, so in our life, too, there come seasons of special opportunity.

The Lord sometimes seems to take forever to respond to our prayers, only to answer many years of prayer all at one go. We stand amazed at all that He is doing, but we must still take care to implement what He is offering us. When God stirs up an interest in spiritual things in someone's life, for example, we must be at hand to introduce them to the Church, and to help them take appropriate action. Opportunities must be seized with both hands, if awakened interest is to mature into fully-fledged discipleship.

Secondly, we cannot move on without commenting once more on the purity of Elijah's motivation throughout this, the longest of days. There are many who pray for fire to come, in the naive assumption that heaven will automatically support their cause. There is a fine line between seeking the kingdom of God and our own self-advancement.

What is quite clear is that Elijah was not in the least

motivated by his own self-interests, but rather by a passionate desire to see God vindicated in the eyes of the watching nation. As He so often does to make the work of intercession authentic, God had inextricably bound His servant's fate to the destiny of the nation. And Elijah was more than willing to place his own life on the line if only God might honour His name with a stunning display of His power. I suspect that if our hearts were similarly motivated we would witness far more works of power than we currently do.

Thirdly, the ecstatic prophets of Baal serve as a warning that mere enthusiasm in religion is no proof of its authenticity. As we shall be considering in the chapter 'The Challenging Counterfeit', spiritual power may come from many sources. It is not only impressionable teenagers, but seemingly solid members of the kingdom, who can be swept away by strange ideas or sudden mid-life crises. The devil strives to inflame our emotions, confuse our minds, ruin our health and damage our reputation.

No matter how exciting some new vision or idea may appear to be, we should give the matter time, and test the spirits before embracing it too readily. Is the hand of heaven really on it? If it is, then we need not attempt to 'whip up' the fire from heaven by our own emotional fervour. We can look to the Lord in full confidence that those who wait on Him shall not be put to shame.

Fourthly, those who claim that the Church has inherited all God's promises for Israel, would do well to ponder the fact that there are more than seventy references to Israel in the New Testament. In all but one of these, it is unequivocally clear that Israel stands for literal Israel, and not for the Church. To substitute the one for the other has been the cause of much needless error and confusion. God selected the Jews for much the same reason that He chose us: to be a demonstration to the world of what He can do through a small, stubborn and insignificant people. And He does not forget His promises![10]

Fifthly, it is salutary to note that many of the most effective prayers of Scripture are extremely short and succinct. Unlike the prolonged ravings of the prophets of Baal, Elijah's prayer for fire to fall was both brief and to the point. It consisted of just two verses and fewer than sixty words. What a contrast to certain prayer meetings we have all endured!

Finally, we can take heart from Elijah's confrontation of the Baals. The episode is a challenge for us not to be afraid to commit ourselves wholeheartedly when the Lord calls us into action against the powers of darkness.

The power of God is able to break through in any situation. Members of Wellspring, the worship group I work with, were ministering recently in the cathedral in Karachi. (There has been much discrimination in Pakistan against the Christian community.) As they prayed for the Spirit of God to come on the gathering, several people outside the building saw flashes of what looked like lightning illuminating the sky around the cathedral.

So impressive were these manifestations that one local witness thought a power station was blowing up! Inside, many were being converted, healed, delivered and filled with the Spirit of God. We can take heart. God will move in power when our prayers stem from a heart that has been touched by His fire. True faith will never be disappointed.[11] Moreover, those who have trusted the Lord in the face of apparent impossibilities acquire a degree of spiritual confidence that blesses other people.

Reflections

God is looking for people who will pray for His fire to fall on situations which may appear as outwardly daunting as that which Elijah faced on Mount Carmel. Specifically lift one or two of these dilemmas to the Lord now.[12]

Selah

Thank You, Lord, for the passion You gave Elijah, and for the clarity of his faith. We ask that You will send this same fire on Your Church. May it burn up confusion and unbelief in our hearts, and set us free from all that has robbed our faith of its clarity. Right now we take our stand against the difficulties that Satan has targeted against us, and ask You to release Your power into the work and visions You have set before us. In Jesus' name, Amen.

References

1. 1 Kings 18:17–19
2. cf Joshua 24:14–27. The Israelites had been vacillating between belief and paganism almost since the day they had left Egypt.
3. 1 Kings 18:21–24; cf Isaiah 55:2, John 6:27. In the Hebrew, to 'waver' means to 'dance' between two opinions.
4. 1 Kings 18:21–24
5. Moses had likewise performed miracles that even the greatest magicians of Egypt had been unable to emulate. The bull, incidentally, was a focus of Baal worship (Genesis 13:8–12; Exodus 7:8–8:19).
6. Revelation 13:13
7. cf Isaiah 14:4–20; Revelation 18
8. 1 Kings 18:36–38. Presumably the water had been specially hauled up the mountainside beforehand.
9. David Pawson once instigated a search around the scene of this incineration. Discovering a fragment of unusually hard rock he sent it away for geological examination. The analyst declared that the fragment, whatever it was, had been exposed to a sudden heat of almost unimaginable temperature!
10. Romans 11:11–29
11. Romans 10:11
12. But be aware that if we are putting anything else in the place of God (our own pleasures, desires, relationships or money) the fire of God will ultimately consume these things! cf 1 Corinthians 3:12–15 and 2 Corinthians 10:3–6.

Chapter 11

The Ministry of Heaven

'And Elijah said to Ahab, "Go and eat and drink, for there is the sound of a heavy rain." So Ahab went off to eat and drink, but Elijah climbed to the top of Carmel, bent down to the ground and put his face between his knees. "Go and look towards the sea," Elijah told his servant. And he went up and looked. "There is nothing there," he said. Seven times Elijah said, "Go back." The seventh time the servant reported, "A cloud as small as a man's hand is rising from the sea." So Elijah said, "Go and tell Ahab, 'Hitch up your chariot and go down before the rain stops you.'" Meanwhile the sky grew black with clouds, the wind rose, a heavy rain came on and Ahab rode off to Jezreel.'

(1 Kings 18:41–45)

Two thousand nine hundred years ago Elijah stood on the top of Mount Carmel and cried out to God for fire to come from heaven. It was a triumph of faith, and a mighty testimony to the power of prayer. Had the contest on Mount Carmel taken a less miraculous turn, Elijah would undoubtedly have perished.

Now that the fire of God had fallen, Elijah longed to see the rains released. One hundred years earlier, the Lord had appeared to Solomon in a dream. He promised the king that if the annual rains were withheld because of sin, then His people must humble themselves, pray and turn from their wicked ways, so that He would hear from heaven and heal their land.[1]

This is an important word for us today. God loves to hear our prayers, and He has made us to be a praying people. Elijah was able to triumph so spectacularly on Mount Carmel because of the earlier spiritual battles he had fought and won. He did not begin praying on the day of the contest itself: he won the victory in the heavenly places while the people were still making their way to the mountain.

There are many in the body of Christ who are prophesying days of revival ahead. There are equally as many who are declaring that God's judgements are coming on us. Which of them is right? Who has stood in the council of the Lord to receive His word?[2]

I believe both messages are true. God is warning us most solemnly that judgement is coming – has indeed already begun in our midst – but that in His mercy, He will still pour out His Spirit on us in abundance. Perhaps we could say that God is looking for reasons by which He may send the grace of revival, rather than the fires of judgement. This is where the concentrated prayers of God's people are vital.[3]

Limitless Power through Prayer

Mark Twain once quipped that he could think of no foreign product which entered his country untaxed except answers to prayer! Unlike any other power in the universe, prayer can cross any distance and release any blockage. There is, quite simply, no limit to what God can accomplish through prayer.

Norman Grubb's biography of the Welsh intercessor, Rees Howells, has helped many to enter new dimensions of prayer. During the Second World War, the Bible College of Wales, which this former miner founded, became a dedicated centre of intercession, exercising a crucial influence over the bearing of world events.

While many books give a brief uplift, the Lord used this particular one to touch the deepest chords in my heart. It was the most stunning confirmation of everything I had already come to believe the Scriptures taught about prayer, for it showed how prayer can affect the lives not only of individuals but also of nations. It was the starting point for many adventures in prayer.[4]

If we are to move in the spirit and power of Elijah, the Church must learn to pray together. We have so much to learn in this respect.[5] Without prayer our life together is shallow. A Chinese preacher declared,

> 'Without prayer, I am like a sea diver cut off from his supply of air; I am a fireman without a hose.'

Elijah knew that the king's heart had not been truly changed by the demonstration of power he had witnessed. He also knew that God was more concerned right then to send rain to the nation, than to deal with Ahab. He therefore urged the king to go and attend to his creature comforts, while he himself climbed again to the summit of Mount Carmel, and prayed for the fulfilment of all that God had promised. While others may be looking for entertainment, the intercessor knows that he, or she, cannot afford to relax until the work is done.

The Power of Compassion

I believe the Church today urgently needs to heed this call to pray. Scripture affords us plenty of examples of urgent prayer, the Lord Jesus Himself being our supreme example.

> *'During the days of Jesus' life on earth, He offered up prayers and petitions with loud cries and tears to the One*

> *who could save Him from death, and He was heard because of His reverent submission.'*[6]

'Cries' translates the Greek *'krauge'*. It is a very strong word which expresses the cry that is wrung from a man under extreme mental or physical distress – such as torture. Here we sound the depths of the compassion of God. No wishy-washy sentimentalized emotion this, but rather a heart-searing, sin-hating, gut-rending plea for mercy to flow where darkness rules, lest judgement and disaster otherwise ensue.

Many of the theological intricacies of prayer will remain forever hidden from us. It is enough for us to know that if the Lord Jesus cried out so often and so loudly in prayer, then we must follow Him along the same path – even if it takes a measure of desperation to drive us to pray in this way. It is when we seek Him with all our hearts that we will find Him.[7]

The Call to Wider Prayer

Elijah's life is a reminder that we are called to share the Lord's wider burdens. As a prophet of the Lord, Elijah had to trust the Lord both for major international issues, and for daily guidance in his own life. The same is true in the ministry of his successor. Just as Elijah had known that he could call down both fire and rain from heaven, so the prophet Elisha would likewise know when his servant Gehazi fell into temptation – not to mention the times when enemies were planning to attack Israel.[8] These men were not psychic; they were simply in close touch with the Lord, who reveals such details to His friends.

There are seasons in the life of prayer just as there are in nature. Elijah was not usually called to the intense degree of spiritual warfare that he experienced on Mount Carmel. Since wrestling is one of the most strenuous forms of exercise known to man, it stands to reason that God will refresh us from our bouts in the wrestling ring by giving us lighter burdens to bear, and times of greater peace and intimacy.[9]

I am left, however, with the uncomfortable impression that many of us have shortened Paul's teaching that we wrestle not against flesh and blood to the more convenient, 'We wrestle not!' Such would certainly appear to be the conclusion of a survey which revealed that the average evangelical spent a dismal three minutes a day in prayer.

I sometimes wonder if much of our busyness is not perilously close to what the New Testament would call worldliness. Which of us would be happy to spend a mere three minutes a day in the company of our dearest friend? Do the interests and priorities of the Kingdom really mean that much to people who ignore them for all but a few seconds a day?

We will be far more fruitful if we can learn to convert information quickly into prayer. Almost every time we meet together as Christians we share matters that are worthy of prayer. Times without number we have found that it is when we say, 'Let's pray together!' (even in the course of telephone conversations) that what had hitherto been an ordinary time of fellowship is transformed into an encounter with the Lord.

Someone once wrote that

> 'prayer is not conquering God's reluctance, but laying hold of His willingness.'

It requires courage and determination to overcome our inner reluctance and to start praying together. There are barriers to overcome, both of enemy opposition and of human embarrassment. But the Lord honours those who persist in the habit of prayer.

Persistence in Prayer

From the summit of Mount Carmel, a lofty watch-tower, Elijah could survey both sea and land. With his head between his knees, his whole demeanour expressed the attitude of a man aware of his continuing dependency. Elijah may have stood boldly before the people, but in the presence of his Maker he could only kneel.[10]

It had required the miracle on Mount Carmel to bring the Israelites to a point where God would again move on their behalf. Now, after three years of longing, Elijah sensed the release in his spirit to pray for God to send the rains and spare the nation.

Tradition has it that the boy who Elijah had raised from the dead grew up to become Elijah's servant: effectively, his adopted son. He would therefore have been the one who ran to the top of Mount Carmel to see if he could see any sign of the promised rain clouds. It is a pleasing and a fitting thought. But put yourself in Elijah's shoes, when this same servant brought him back a negative report six times in a row. Would you not have found it easy to fall into the expectation that nothing was ever going to change?

I consider it highly significant that Elijah had to send his servant back no fewer than seven times. Just as his stay by Cherith and Zarephath had been a prolonged one, so there was to be no instant victory even now. The best things in life do not come easily.

Failing to understand this, many have allowed delays and disappointments to discourage them from going further along the intercessory path. But why should the Lord always answer our prayers the first time round? Do not His delays teach us to look even more fervently to Him? Surely the Lord waits to be gracious to us![11]

If we did not need to persevere in prayer we would soon become self-sufficient. A great deal depends, therefore, on our willingness to refuse the pangs of discouragement that come our way, and to keep praying on until the power of God breaks through.

Shortly after my conversion I felt a burden to pray for an old school friend. My clumsy and ineffective attempts to witness to her met with no success, and for the next twelve years I lost all contact with her. Indeed, I often wondered how much my prayers really were the leading of the Lord, and how much they were just my own desire to see her come to the Lord.

Over the years, however, the burden regularly returned, so I continued to pour out my heart to God. One night, I dreamt that she had committed her life to Christ. I shared this with Rosalind, hoping, but by no means convinced, that it might be true. The very next day we received a letter from her (the first in over twelve years) letting me know she had recently been converted, and had already led several people in her village to the Lord!

How good God is, not only to answer our prayers, but even to let us know that they have been answered. One of the great surprises of prayer is that we never know what God will accomplish through it. I had thought I was praying for one person, little suspecting that she herself would become a fervent soul-winner. The destiny of many other people is bound up in the prayers we pray.

Breakthrough

Revivals are less the fruit of good techniques than of groups of people covenanting with the Lord and with each other to pray, and to keep laying hold of God until the heavens open and souls are saved.

In 1858 a great revival broke out on both sides of the Atlantic. It is, perhaps, less talked about today than the earlier one in John Wesley's day, but it added a million people to the Kingdom in Great Britain within the space of a year, and revived a further million within the Church. There were no big-name speakers; it was a 'grass-roots' movement which began with groups of people coming together to pray.

The powerful work of Teen Challenge that David Wilkerson pioneered among drug addicts, likewise owes its origins to prayer. This simple country pastor made a crucial decision to turn his television set off, and to spend the final two hours of the day instead in prayer.

Or take the example of a missionary called James Fraser. Despite the repeated discouragement of seeing not a single soul attending his meetings, Fraser kept on praying, year after year, for the Lisu tribe. His astonishing determination 'not just to rest in the faithfulness of God' (the armchair mentality) but to take hold of the faithfulness of God to secure big results for God kept him believing the specific promises of God's word. And how his faithfulness was rewarded! The power of God broke through, and a wonderful and far-reaching revival touched the Lisu tribe.[12]

The chances are that we ourselves have come to know the Lord Jesus because someone prayed for us. I know that I owe my own salvation in no small measure to the power of intercession. The Lord told the people leading the student mission in which I became a Christian that they would reap a great harvest if they would rise in the night to pray for souls. Over one hundred and fifty of us committed our lives to the Lord during that week. Many are now in full-time service for the Lord.

I think of another friend, who has long exercised a worldwide ministry. While he was still a boy, a missionary visited his school and felt led to promise that he would pray for him every day. Through a 'chance' meeting eighteen years later the missionary was able to see at first hand the ministry he had been so instrumental in praying into being.

Though he could have had no way of knowing it, his prayers for one obscure school boy would one day lead thousands of people, in places as far apart as America and Indonesia, to a knowledge of the Lord Jesus. The missionary was faithful to his call, and he will have his reward. So too will we, as we give ourselves to the ministry of prayer.

Burden Bearing in Prayer

The life of prayer requires perspective as well as persistence. If we feel as though we are not getting through on some particular issue, it is often helpful to try approaching it from some other angle. For example, if you have been getting no answer to the prayer, 'Shall I do such and such, Lord?' why not try phrasing it the other way round? 'Lord, is there any reason why I should not do this?' He will not fail to warn us if we are in serious danger of going off course. The change of angle often makes all the difference.[13]

As a man of like passions to ourselves, we can imagine that Elijah must have wrestled with all sorts of misgivings as he looked up at the cloudless sky. Just as he had faced and conquered the temptation to worry about whether the ravens would come to feed him, now he had to trust the Lord to send rain from a cloudless sky. What a fool he would look in Ahab's eyes if nothing happened!

Resolute against these plaguing thoughts, Elijah laid hold of God's Word with that peculiar combination of boldness and urgency that is the hallmark of the true intercessor. The sight of the merest wisp of cloud far out to sea was enough to convince him: God was about to answer his prayers and fulfil His word. He promptly sent his servant to warn Ahab to set out before he was stranded by the flash-floods that would soon be on them. The proud monarch, who clearly trusted Elijah's insight more than he feared Elijah's God, obeyed without hesitation.

The Lord is looking for His people to come forward and offer themselves to stand in the gap for the welfare of this land.[14] He has granted us the immense privilege of being able to win God's blessing for others through prayer, and so extend His kingdom. The Lord wants this to be a living adventure for us, and to give us joy in His house of prayer.

Reflections

The Lord Jesus *'is at the right hand of God, interceding for us.'*[15] Through prayer we are permitted to share in the ministry of heaven. Amin Gesswein wrote,

> 'Our generation has yet to see prayer as a ministry, and to take God at His word on this subject. It is while we pray that God works, not merely before or after prayer ... Prayer is our real work.'

Talk to the Lord about the quality of your prayer life. What specific burdens has He given you? Have you been faithful to them? Pray to make your own home, and church, 'a house of prayer for all nations.'[16]

Selah

> Lord, I want to take this call to prayer seriously. Forgive me for putting other pursuits and concerns ahead of seeking You. Forgive me too for not wanting to pay the cost involved in seeking You. I cannot change myself, but I am willing to be changed. Here and now I ask for the gift of faith-filled intercession. Grant that my authority and anointing in prayer may increase from one year to the next. May I pray the prayers You most desire me to pray, and take the opportunities You send to pray with others. I ask this for the glory of God, and in Jesus' name. Amen.

References

1. 2 Chronicles 7:12–15
2. Jeremiah 23:18
3. cf Isaiah 56:7; Joel 2:15–18; 2 Chronicles 20:4; Ezra 10:7; Acts 4:23–31, 12:12
4. *Rees Howells, Intercessor*, by Norman Grubb (Lutterworth Press). Another book I would recommend on the subject is *Prayer*, by Oles Hallesby (IVP).
5. I wrote *Explaining Praying Together* (Sovereign World) to help Christians understand more of the dynamics, as well as the possibilities, that are available to us through corporate prayer.
6. Hebrews 5:7
7. Jeremiah 29:12–13
8. See 2 Kings 5:25–27 and 2 Kings 6:8–12 for examples of the Lord making Elisha dramatically aware of the enemy's plans.
9. It is also worth saying that people's capacity to bear burdens is very different, and that it varies from one phase of our life to another. A right understanding of this will help to avoid overloading either ourselves or each other.
10. It has been pointed out that this is a classic birthing position. Elijah was giving birth to the rains that would save the nation; cf Galatians 4:19.
11. Isaiah 30:18
12. See *The Prayer of Faith*, by James Fraser (OMF).
13. Isaiah 30:21
14. Ezekiel 22:30–31
15. Romans 8:34; cf Hebrews 7:25
16. Isaiah 56:7

Chapter 12

The Importance of Rest

'The power of the Lord came upon Elijah and, tucking his cloak into his belt, he ran ahead of Ahab all the way to Jezreel.' (1 Kings 18:46)

Elijah had reached the high point of his ministry. He had stood before the nation and prayed down the fire of God on the sacrifice. All who were present had witnessed a startling demonstration that Yahweh was more powerful than Baal, and the news soon travelled throughout the nation. Neither the people, nor the king would ever be quite the same again after the dramatic events of that day.

Unfortunately, neither would the prophet himself. Elijah had reckoned without the effect of this victory on his own character. Success is a great deal harder to handle than most of us have realised. So many strive for it, never pausing to ponder the character, as well as the effort, that will be required to sustain it. As Philip Keller points out, there are few, very few, who can live with such anointing and yet remain completely humble and dependent on the Lord.[1]

I can do no more than repeat, for my own benefit if for no one else's, that pride is a most subtle foe. It is the hallmark of our enemy, the true reflection of his heart. It may take the form of a desire to be rich and famous – or perhaps to feel superior to others, but in whatever guise it assails us we must be careful. Lucifer is prepared to trade success for a foothold in our soul.

In the excitement of the moment, it was as though Elijah suddenly longed to throw off all the constraints and hardships he had been subjected to during his hidden years as an outcast. After all, now that the prophets of Baal had been defeated, why should the king not recognise his part in the proceedings? Surely even so hard-hearted a man as Ahab must have been impressed by what the Lord had done on Mount Carmel!

At such an exalted moment, Elijah found it hard to believe that God had chosen to keep him hidden from the public eye, not only because the situation called for it, but also for the good of his own soul. But as we shall be seeing, it is precisely because he did not take time to rest and recover after the huge outlay of mental and spiritual energy in the battle on Mount Carmel, that he was so vulnerable in the immediate aftermath.

Uncommanded Works

For the first time in the scriptural account, we find Elijah acting without a specific command of the Lord. What was there really to be gained by rushing off to visit the stronghold of his enemy? Was he not simply eager to see how the queen would react when she heard the news that her beloved prophets had been overthrown?

Not everyone will agree with me on this point, but I am tempted to wonder whether Elijah did not misuse the power of the Lord, by running ahead of His anointing. Most of us have experienced moments when an almost supernatural strength seems to flow through us while we are engaged on some special project. But we should not confuse adrenalin with anointing.

Moreover, Elijah had spent a whole day without food. Might he not have responded differently in the crisis he was about to experience had he had something to eat first? Scripture has much to say about the value of fasting, but it also reveals that there is such a thing as inappropriate fasting.[2]

Fasting shows the Lord that we are willing to make sacrifices in order to reach some God-given goal. It frees the soul to enter more deeply into the spiritual conflict, and it sharpens our ability to identify with people in need. It is something most of us need to learn more about. Yet, for all the many benefits we derive from fasting, it is as well to be aware that it may also serve to open us to a higher degree of temptation, precisely because it weakens our normal defence mechanisms.[3]

Much though we are called to wrestle for the kingdom, there is also a time to rest from our labours and to enjoy complete freedom from our usual burdens. If we are the sort of people who pick up everybody's concerns whenever we attend a meeting, then life risks becoming altogether too serious. It is not unspiritual to take time off; indeed, we will often find that our best ideas come when we are at our most relaxed.

Non-Burden-Bearing Times

Years ago, as an eager young Christian worker, I used to feel mildly guilty at taking a day off a week. Partly this was due to not wanting to miss out on all the Lord was doing, but also because I felt embarrassed at being able to relax at times when others were working. Today, after experiencing the blessings of countless days off, I have come to realise that these non-burden-bearing times are less a luxury God indulges me with, than an integral part of His purposes for my life.

Relaxation is important for the soul, especially if it be a rest towards God, rather than a rest from Him. Escapist retreats into a fantasy world hinder our spiritual development, because they create a highly-coloured expectation of what life ought to be like. Against such impossibly high and misleading standards, ordinary everyday life is bound to appear almost unbearably drab.

We have spoken earlier about our need to pay attention to the pace at which we lead our lives. So many today are experiencing at least some of the symptoms of burn-out: shallow breathing, restless nights, poor digestion and wayward thoughts. More contact time with the Lord, and consequently less with the source of our tension, may well be a key to recovery.

Piercing the Darkness

Sooner or later almost everyone who ministers for the Lord reaches a point where they feel so far down that they wonder if they will ever come up again. Like Elijah, there is a danger of turning in on ourselves at such times, pitying our plight rather than considering the power of the Lord. Our need at such times is exactly the same as Elijah's – a deeper repentance and a fresh touch from the living Lord.

I am grateful that Scripture is so faithful in recording the 'downside' of its heroes. It would be unthinkable in the Koran, for example, to depict the prophets of Allah falling into error or deception. In the Bible, by contrast, great men sometimes fail spectacularly – and become still more real and accessible to us through doing so.

What, for example, could be more disreputable than Abraham, who lied to his host, Moses who killed a man in a brawl, or David who murdered the husband of a woman he had decided on an impulse to take to bed? As for Peter, the less said the better – denying his Lord only hours after swearing that he would never do such a thing!

It is wonderful how God fashioned leaders after His own heart out of such abysmal failures. People who have been deeply humbled walk a great deal more circumspectly in the fear of the Lord. Indeed, I sometimes think that most true success is built out of 'failure' of one kind or another.

What a comfort it is to realise that God can always pick us up one more time than we can fall. It would be hard to imagine anything further from today's propensity to discard the failures than the delightful way in which the Lord restores His servant.

Because we may find Elijah's dark days mirrored in our own experience, I believe it will be helpful for us to follow Elijah through this low point in his pilgrimage. We will stand alongside him as he wrestles with the shock of Jezebel's threat against his life, empathize as waves of condemnation and despondency assail him, and finally rejoice as he is recommissioned for further service.

Reflections

What steps are you taking to ensure sufficient non-burden-bearing times in your own life? Is there anything you can do to adjust the pace of your life? Ask the Lord to show you if there are areas where you are going beyond what He has asked you to do.

> *'Let the beloved of the Lord rest secure in Him, for He shields him all day long, and the one the Lord loves rests between His shoulders.'* (Deuteronomy 33:12)

Selah

Lord, as we realise how badly Elijah needed rest at this time in his life, we know You do not want us to overstretch ourselves. Help us to live within our emotional means, and to take advantage of quieter times to recharge our batteries.

Help us to know that we are acceptable to You, whether or not we have accomplished all we long to do.

Take from our hearts all roots of rejection, and all seeds of striving. Save us, and all Your precious servants, from the perils of perfectionism, and the turmoil of burn-out. In Jesus' name, Amen.

References

1. Philip Keller's book, *Power* (Bridge Publishing) is the most readable account of Elijah's life I have come across. I would commend any of this sensitive man's outstanding writings.
2. 1 Samuel 14:24–31
3. Arthur Wallis' book, *God's Chosen Fast* (Kingsway) has become a classic on the subject.

Chapter 13

Strategic Retreat or Headlong Flight?

'Now Ahab told Jezebel everything Elijah had done and how he had killed all the prophets with the sword. So Jezebel sent a messenger to Elijah to say, "May the gods deal with me, be it ever so severely, if by this time tomorrow I do not make your life like that of one of them." Elijah was afraid and ran for his life. When he came to Beersheba in Judah, he left his servant there, while he himself went a day's journey into the desert.'

(1 Kings 19:1–4)

We can easily imagine the scene as the king returned home. Ahab may have been impressed by what he had seen, but he lacked the courage to mention the Lord's part in the dramatic happenings on Mount Carmel. As far as he was concerned (at least, when faced by his wife's commanding presence) it was Elijah alone who had caused all the trouble.

What damage the enemy causes through the seemingly gentle ties of mistaken affection! Ahab, who was clearly as fascinated by Elijah as Herod was by John the Baptist, might well have opened his heart to the Lord – had it not already been devoted to Jezebel. Now, as he made his report, he quailed before her anger. 'What do you mean you let him escape? Why did you organise a contest when you had the man in your power? Things would have turned out differently if I'd been there!'

From this distance in history – and especially because we know the end of the story – it is tempting to view Jezebel's threats against Elijah much as we would the Red Queen's blusterings in Alice in Wonderland. Both creatures were wont to shout 'Off with his head' at the slightest provocation. But it would be naive to underestimate this formidable opponent, whose cruelty had already taken such a toll on the life of the nation.

Like the forty Jews who vowed they would not eat until Paul had been assassinated, Jezebel vowed that Elijah should pay for the blood of her prophets with his own life. In her craving for revenge, Jezebel becomes the image and forerunner of a thousand latter-day persecutors of the saints. She did not realise that she had sided with the prince of darkness, and so had sealed her own fate.

The Weight of Suffering

Jezebel's wholesale slaughter of the prophets of the Lord – and Obadiah's heroic attempts to protect them – have an ominously familiar ring at the end of this blood-soaked twentieth century. More people have died for their faith in these supposedly enlightened days than in all the preceding centuries put together.[1]

Tertullian's comment, 'The blood of martyrs is the seed of the Church,' reminds us that to be a 'witness' for the Lord can also mean, in the original Greek, to be a 'martyr'. This being so, it is more important than ever for us to know that God's love is stronger than death. His light will ultimately dispel all darkness. As Kierkegaard wrote,

> 'The tyrant dies and his reign ends; the martyr dies and his rule begins.'

Ours too is an age in which it sometimes seems as though evil has been given the power to overcome, even as it appeared to have defeated the cause of Yahweh in Elijah's day.[2] It must have felt that way when the Muslim Turks overran Asia Minor, and then destroyed the Church throughout North Africa during the Dark Ages. Still to this day the reign of the crescent continues to dwarf the cross in these regions. Islam is so rampantly on the offensive as a military-religious-economic force that the very fate of the Church in the Middle East appears to be in the balance.

Because the Lord is at the centre of His Church, however, there is always hope, not only for its continuing survival, but even for a mighty harvest of souls. This is God's hour to reach many Muslims with the love of Jesus – even as His hour had come to touch Israel through a stirring demonstration of His power.

In Western societies, too, those who are seeking to be true to Christ are facing pressure of many kinds. Our 'democratic' system of unthinking consumerism has strayed so far from God's pattern for our lives that we are just as much in need of God's prophetic challenge as any more obviously anti-Christian form of government.

When we see the corruption that is at the heart of so many of today's world systems, it is no wonder it causes our spirits great distress. We shall consider later how the Lord can help us to convert these feelings into deep mourning and effective prayer.

Surprise Attack

The Scriptures warn that:

> *'...all who ... are determined to live a devoted and godly life in Christ Jesus will meet with persecution – that is, will be made to suffer because of their religious stand.'*[3]

You may not find this verse featured in your 'Promise Box,' but there are many other New Testament texts which point to the same truth.[4]

The powers of darkness are resilient, and have enormous resources to call on. They are ever on the watch to find fresh occasions to disturb our peace, and to damage the cause for which we are fighting. We are never more vulnerable than in our moments of greatest triumph. In the relief that follows a time of immense strain, we are prone to let our defences down.

'Kick-back' is a ferocious weapon. David Watson and Charles Spurgeon both recorded that they were never more prone to feelings of dejection than after they had finished preaching. Having given themselves so fully to their task, they had little left with which to face the fresh challenges the enemy directed their way.

Mountaineers experience pain not only as they battle through the thin air to reach the summit, but still more as they begin their descent. Incredibly, soldiers may be unaware that they have been shot in the heat of battle. The shock and the pain come later.

Much has been written as to whether or not Elijah did the right thing in running away. The point is that Jezebel's threat reached Elijah at a time when he was already exhausted. Since God rarely works miracles on behalf of those who persistently refuse to take ordinary human precautions, it could be argued that this was a necessary flight. He was, after all facing a real threat to his life. Were Elijah to be killed now, the forces of Baal would register a stunning counterattack and quickly make up for their recent humiliation.

All such reasoning is perfectly plausible, but the tenor of Scripture points elsewhere. We are clearly told that Elijah was afraid and ran for his life. For once, his faith failed him and he fell prey to that fear of man which is such a snare to the soul.[5] From having shown practically no concern for his own self-interests in the past, he found himself now overwhelmed with fears for his own survival.

Perhaps it is easier to hold the prospect of death more lightly when we have little left to lose. It is a much more daunting foe when victory, and better prospects, are within our sights. Nevertheless, as servants of the Lord, we are not free to desert our posts when the going gets tough. Elijah's physical presence was badly needed to maintain the impetus of the reformation. The writer of Ecclesiastes advises,

> *'If a ruler's anger rises against you, do not leave your post; calmness can lay great errors to rest.'*[6]

Driven to the Desert

Jezebel's threat hit Elijah so hard that he forgot all the times the Lord had rescued him in the past; forgot, too, the golden principle he had hitherto practised, of consulting the Lord before embarking on any new course of action.

The sad sight of Elijah plunging into the scorching wilderness, and running until he dropped, is a poignant reminder that there are bound to be consequences when leaders lose their confidence. We can only imagine what Elijah's servant must have felt as his master turned tail and fled. It is, perhaps, a reminder that we dare not put our ultimate trust in any person, no matter how strong they may appear. We do each other no favours when we demand too much of our leaders.

Elijah reached the land of Judah, but he dared not stay there. King Jehoshaphat had allied himself through his daughter's marriage to Ahab's son, and the prophet feared a diplomatic extradition. Thoughtfully leaving his servant behind to spare him witnessing his extreme misery, Elijah hurried on until he came to the southern desert. There he lay down under a broom tree, and cried aloud for the Lord to take him home.

Would Elijah have fared better had he stood firm and trusted the Lord to deliver him from Jezebel? We cannot know for certain, because history records that God has a different solution for every dilemma. When Elisha found himself besieged by his attackers, he made no attempt to run away. He was so confident that the host of heaven was with him that he did not even need to see the angels who were protecting him; he merely prayed for his servant to be able to see them. Elisha's astonishing faith saved the city.[7]

There have been instances when the Lord's servants have set out on a course of action, knowing full well the suffering that will follow. We think of Paul, for instance, as he journeyed to Jerusalem, well warned by both the Lord and His people of the sufferings ahead.[8] On the other hand, we can point to other occasions when circumstances necessitated a hasty flight from danger. Saul, for example, was warned to flee from Damascus, just as Mary and Joseph were told to take the baby Jesus to Egypt.[9]

The history of the Church shows the same dichotomy. Demos Shakarian relates how wonderfully blessed were the Armenians who obeyed the Lord's warnings and fled to America. Those who stayed behind suffered the most appalling persecution.[10]

There can no more be a simple right or wrong course of action to follow at such times, therefore, than there can be a blanket answer to the question, 'Should I stay in or out of the historical churches when there is so much false teaching in them?' Each situation requires us to seek God afresh, and to follow whatever advice or example He gives us.

Sometimes it is a choice not between right and wrong but rather between two evils. Richard Wurmbrand records how he had to tell many lies during his daily interrogations in a Romanian torture chamber in order to protect other members of the underground church. If he had told the literal truth, many innocent lives would have been lost. May the Lord spare us from ever being placed in such a situation

– but may He give us the wisdom we will need should such a time ever come upon us![11]

At the end of the day, I find it hard to escape the conclusion that Elijah would have been wiser never to have gone to Jezreel in the first place. If he had sought out somewhere quiet in order to recharge his body with food, and his spiritual batteries with prayer, then he would have been far better prepared for the next round of the battle. But then I reflect on all the wisdom and encouragement I have gained precisely because Elijah did go through such a dark time, and I smile. God understands us so well. He knows how we will respond, and He uses even our mistakes for His own purposes and glory.

In the meantime, however, Elijah had to come face to face with an almost overwhelming sense of failure. Some of us will recognise this powerful emotion only too well – and how we handle it is all important. We either cry out to the Lord to turn seemingly impossible situations around for His glory, or we become bogged down in the quagmires of self-pity, bitterness, doubt and unforgiveness.

Most of us agree, in a relatively unthinking head-nodding way, that forgiveness is a right and proper idea – until we have something major to forgive. The problem then is that we may succeed in cloaking our resentment to the point where we all but deceive ourselves.

There is only one letter difference between the words 'repent' and 'resent', yet all the difference in the world in their outworking. Resentment is not an automatic response to a disappointment: it too is a choice. Every victory we gain over these foes defeats the enemy's attempt to induce blockages in our hearts, and represents a notable step forward for the Kingdom.

Reflections

The great revivalist Finney taught that nothing can stop

God's purposes for us – provided only that we are willing to forgive. Who is it we need to forgive most often? Our friends and family of course!

Honesty is essential if we are to respond to difficulties with faith, rather than with resentment or flight. Think of people who, as you perceive it, have hurt or failed you. Pray for the Lord to redeem these bitter situations, as well as to cleanse your own memories of them.

If you feel upset because God has allowed some disappointment to come your way, 'forgive' Him for allowing it to happen. It clears the air wonderfully!

Surround the people concerned with the healing love and forgiveness of God. It is impossible to fear or resent someone you have chosen to love. As William Law put it,

> 'There is nothing which makes us love a man so much as praying for him!'

Equally, you may need to forgive yourself for the way you are, or the manner in which you reacted to a specific situation. Take an example of an occasion when, as you perceive it, you let yourself (or others) down. Bathe the person you were then in the love-light of Christ, forgiving yourself just as you would forgive anyone else. Then you will be better prepared for the next test of faith!

Selah

> Lord, thank You that You are the God of new beginnings. Thank You that You do not give up on us. Forgive us when we have been foolish and unforgiving, too ready to blame others, and too slow to humble ourselves. Help us not to run away from our failures, but to receive Your forgiveness, even as we forgive those who have let us down.

I give you especially the matter of . . . .
Please turn even this around for Your glory.

Grant me opportunities, Lord, to help restore those who are hurting, and who feel tempted like Elijah, to run away. In Jesus' name, Amen.

References

1. To see how true this is, we have only to look at the suffering Christians are enduring not only in the remaining communist countries – of which China is by far the chief example – but also among the forty-three officially Muslim nations. See John 15:18ff.
2. Revelation 13:7–18; cf Daniel 7:20–22
3. 2 Timothy 3:12 Amplified
4. e.g. Matthew 10:22; John 15:20, 16:2; Acts 9:16, 14:22; 1 Corinthians 4:10; Hebrews 10:33; 2 Timothy 1:8, 2:3; Revelation 2:10; Romans 8:17; cf Matthew 16:21, 17:22, 20:17; John 10:17–18
5. Proverbs 29:25; cf Isaiah 51:12–16; John 12:42–43; Galatians 2:11–14
6. Ecclesiastes 10:4
7. 2 Kings 6:15–16
8. Acts 21:10–14
9. Acts 9:25; Matthew 2:13
10. See *The Happiest People on Earth*, by Demos Shekarian (Hodder).
11. See the chapter 'The Absolute Necessity of Truthfulness' in *Alone with God*, by Richard Wurmbrand (Hodder).

Chapter 14

Shock and Shame

'"May the gods deal with me, be it ever so severely, if by this time tomorrow I do not make your life like that of one of them." Elijah was afraid and ran for his life.'
(1 Kings 19:2–3)

In his public and prophetic life, Elijah appears such a giant of a man that it is easy to forget he was a man of like passions to ourselves, and therefore every bit as susceptible to discouragement as we are. Accustomed as he was to the silence of a withdrawn lifestyle, it had cost Elijah a great deal of emotional energy to spend a whole day defying the crazed and demented prophets of Baal. Now, like a weary kangaroo, he was 'out of bounds,' and ready to give in.

Knox translates potently what happened next:

> 'Elijah took fright and set out upon a journey of his own devising.'

During his stay by the brook Cherith, and again in Zarephath, Elijah had at least been able to comfort himself with the thought that it had been God who had placed him there. It is a hundred times more humbling to find ourselves in a wilderness of our own making!

Jezebel's challenge had shaken Elijah to the core of his

being. One woman's threats achieved what the combined might of the prophets of Baal had failed to do: to remove him from the stage. It is a tragic sequel to a day that had begun outstandingly well – and a powerful reminder of how surprise can lead to shock, which in turn can lead to flight.

The Neurosis of Faith

Those who have never experienced any real shock, let alone the pangs of anxiety, may have difficulty relating to this episode in Elijah's life. But whether or not Elijah's extreme weakness at this time has any immediate application in our own life, I believe we can learn valuable lessons about the way shock works by studying his brief collapse of trust.

To be on the front line for the Lord means receiving many blows and woundings from the rulers of this present world. When we lose loved ones, or our health, work or ministry take a turn for the worse, it is no wonder if our mind races as we struggle to come to terms with the unthinkable.

Neither does it necessarily take anything so radical as the loss of a partner, or a job, for our mind to cross over the boundaries into shock. Any form of loss or change may cause this to happen, especially if a number of different pressures come our way at the same time.

Perhaps if we were more aware of the multitudes who lie awake at night in prey to anxious thoughts, then our hearts would be more compassionate. Fear of failure, fear of rejection, fear of the future, fear even of what God Himself will ask of us ... These are giants that only grace can assuage and faith finally slay.

Unpleasant though the outward symptoms of anxiety are – the shallow breathing, heart palpitations, stomach aches, sudden bursts of cold sweat and shaking – they are ultimately less pernicious than the way in which shock can paralyse our trust. Just as the body takes time to heal after an injury, so we must give ourselves, and others, the grace and space in which to adjust and recover.

Coping with Shock

The first and all-important step is to realise when we are at risk. To live with unacknowledged shock in our system (or repressed grief for that matter) is as potentially dangerous as holding unexploded gelignite in our hands. If we are not bringing our wounded emotions into the healing love-light of Jesus, there is a constant risk that circumstances may cause us either to explode, spiting others in the process, or to implode, pushing us deeper into ourselves. Honesty, with ourselves and with the Lord, can cure anything. The second thing to hold on to, therefore, is our confidence that He can handle our problems!

Satan had played his master stroke, and it had hurt Elijah deeply. But as another prophet cried out,

> *'Do not gloat over me, my enemy! Though I have fallen, I will rise. Though I sit in darkness, the Lord will be my light.'*[1]

The Lord is not angry with us if we feel disheartened, or when our confidence collapses. The apostle commands us to

> *'Be merciful to those who doubt.'*[2]

We must apply this principle to our own lives too, and be as gentle as we would wish others to be with us. If we are too hard on ourselves, we will merely intensify our feelings of alienation, and effectively condemn ourselves to respond in the same way again when a similar set of circumstances comes our way.

Even though our background and spiritual sense of responsibility may make it hard for us to admit how we are really feeling, this is no time to adopt the stiff upper lip. What we pray at such times may sound as hopelessly untheological as Elijah's cry to be allowed to die, but the fact that we are pouring out our heart to God is important. At the end of the day, God honoured Job, who protested loudly that human sinfulness is not the only reason for our suffering, rather than his pious companions, who set out to comfort their friend, but who ended up wounding him with wrongful accusations.[3]

If the line between self-pity and a genuine heart cry is sometimes a fine one, the Lord errs on the side of generosity. Just as we encourage our children to share their hurts and troubles with us, so it is good for us to pour out our heartfelt feelings to the Lord. We are not backsliding, we are hurting, and God understands hurt. If we need to tell the Lord the same thing over and over again, then let us not be afraid to do so. This is not idle repetition: it is a necessary stage in taking the healing process from head to heart. The Lord is with us, and He will not get tired of hearing our cries.

It pays to learn from experience which attitudes and actions help the recovery process, and which hinder it. For while certain types of company, and activity, may help to draw us closer to the Lord, others will distract and distance us from Him.

We are not backsliding if we need to concentrate on less demanding pursuits and engagements for a while. To add the strain of additional responsibilities at a time when we are already emotionally overstretched is rarely wise. We are better off taking plenty of rest, and steadying ourselves with soothing truths and undemanding friends. Books and music that will comfort and restore our spirits will also help, as will plenty of fresh air, and busying ourselves with practical tasks.

Be assured that your experience is not unique. Countless Christians have been through the sort of crisis that Elijah experienced, and can testify how the Lord has used these times of surprise and shock as a means of leading them to know the Lord in a deeper way.

While we are in that first stage of heart-pounding shock, however, it is all too easy to press the panic button, and to make impulsive statements and decisions that we will later regret. Our first reactions are rarely mature ones, any more than Elijah's were in this instance. We do well to bear in mind that

> *'He that believes shall not make haste.'*[4]

If at all possible, avoid taking irreversible steps; now is rarely the best moment to make life-changing decisions. At all costs beware of festering over-introspection, which tries too hard to pin-point the reasons for whatever we are experiencing. Since these may only become clearer to us with hindsight – if at all – peace will come more through yielding than by demanding answers. His presence will not fail to be with us day by day while we wait for clarity to come.

Riding the Waves

In earthquake zones the danger of aftershocks is well known. It is much the same with human and spiritual shakings, as shock waves return again and again, threatening to engulf us. Let me share something I have found helpful in combating the onset of these horrible emotions. When I am aware of the first stirrings of shock and anxiety rising in my heart, I try to convert their strongly negative power into a fervent prayer that affirms the opposite of whatever it is that is being suggested.

The secret is to catch the thoughts, rather like a surfer, who needs to ride just ahead of the crest of the wave. If the surfer gets the timing wrong, the waves will roll over and submerge him, just as these emotions threaten to swamp us. But if we ride the waves, we can harness their power through prayer and accomplish more than if they had never come our way.

I hate shocks every bit as much as anyone else. Yet I am forced to recognise that my own life, like that of the wider Church, has grown as a result of pressure. The Lord works in mysterious ways to transform our griefs and disappointments into His 'appointments' as we cry out to Him. He knew exactly what He was doing when He brought us into His Kingdom, and He knows where He is leading us. Like the Psalmist, we will be able to testify,

> *'When anxiety was great within me, Your consolation brought joy to my soul.'*[5]

Reflections

Take to heart these words Sir Thomas More penned, as coming from the Lord:

> 'Pluck up thy courage, faint heart . . . for I Myself have vanquished the whole world, and yet felt I far more fear, sorrow, weariness, and much more inward anguish too, when I considered My most bitter passion. But thou, now, O timorous and weak silly sheep, think it sufficient for thee only to walk after Me, which am thy Shepherd and Governor, and so mistrust thyself and put thy trust in Me. Take hold of the hem of My garment, therefore.'

Selah[6]

> Thank You, Lord, that You understand when we are knocked off-balance. I ask You to help all who are suffering today from the after-effects of any kind

of shock: from accident or disappointment, from bereavement or bewilderment. Be with each one, dear Lord, and send them Your comfort in the way that will best minister to them. Free them from the after-effects of all their shocks. Restore their heart to love and trust, their mind to think and act creatively, and their will to serve.

Lead our steps to those who are suffering, and make us a source of refreshment to the bruised and weary. In Jesus' name, Amen.

References

1. Micah 7:8
2. Jude 22
3. Job 5:10–16, 12:13–25
4. Isaiah 28:16 KJV
5. Psalm 94:29; cf Psalms 62:5–8, 27:1–2; 2 Corinthians 10:5. It has also been said that though we may often be hurt in the service of the Kingdom, we will rarely be seriously harmed.
6. You may find it helpful to substitute 'me' for 'all', and 'us' and 'our' for 'them' and 'their' to make this prayer applicable to your own situation.

Chapter 15

The Temptation to Despair

'Elijah ... went a day's journey into the desert. He came to a broom tree, sat down under it and prayed that he might die. "I have had enough, Lord," he said. "Take my life. I am no better than my ancestors."'

(1 Kings 19:4)

How alone Elijah felt as he pursued his headlong flight into the desert. We find him, slumped beneath a tree in the desert, a despairing prayer on his lips. Behind his cry, a fierce spiritual battle was raging. The powers of darkness were closing in, assailing the battered prophet with lies and self-accusations, until he succumbed to the hammer blows of Satan's attacks, and ended up believing something that was not true: namely, that he was worse than he really was.

What was behind Elijah's desire to run away? It was certainly not being on his own that was the problem, for we have seen already how wonderfully at home Elijah could be in the presence of the Lord. No, it was his motivation that had collapsed.

Elijah was suffering from a combination of exhaustion, despair and condemnation – that terrible condition which plagues the majority of Christians at some time or another, and which makes us feel an outsider to God's goodness.

So long as Elijah had looked at the Lord, he had

triumphed over impossible situations and fearsome odds. As soon as he looked at his own peril, however, he found himself unable to respond to this latest threat against his life.

The Cost of Taking a Stand

The love of God had constrained Elijah to go and confront Ahab, but there is a price to pay once we begin challenging vested interests and evil strongholds. To plead for causes that are too righteous to be popular, to tell a compromised Church that it is corrupt, and to strive to awaken slumbering consciences has always been the prophet's arduous task. Anyone whose duty has led him to challenge prevailing opinion will know the anguish of such isolation – but they also know that it would be quite wrong not to take such a stand.[1]

What breakthroughs of God's Spirit might never have occurred if the apostles had not withstood the Sanhedrin, if John Wycliffe and William Tyndale had not pursued God's plan to translate the Bible into English, if Martin Luther had not defied the Pope, and if John Wesley had not 'consented to be more vile' and preach the gospel in the open air?

It is not uncommon for pioneers of faith to feel forsaken at their time of greatest need. Our Lord Himself was treated thus. One plus God is a majority, but we may still face times when we feel overwhelmed by circumstances. Even Moses lost his cool at one point, and smashed the stone tablets of the law. So too did David, when, in a moment of rank despair, he ran away to join the Philistine army.[2]

The Prophet's Despair

Despite the victory on Mount Carmel, it felt to Elijah as though nothing much had changed. The people may have witnessed the power of God, but they were by no means converted. As for Jezebel, she still sat securely on her throne. Why had God hinted at so much, but accomplished so little? The powers of darkness crowded in, eager to convince the exhausted prophet that all his efforts had been in vain.

As all hope of accomplishing anything useful withered in Elijah's heart, it seemed to him that he was no better than his ancestors. For one terrible moment he found himself forced to consider the unthinkable: that he had been mistaken all along in believing that he had been chosen for the task of drawing the nation back to God. In the agony of that tortured awareness, a dark cloud of despair settled on him: the past appeared to have been wasted, the present was unbearable, and the future too bleak to contemplate. Elijah cried out that he might be allowed to die.

It is not as unusual as one might imagine to come across a Jeremiah cursing the day that he was born, or an Elijah asking to be allowed to die. Extreme pressure often has the effect of making burden-bearers want to quit. We must be careful. If we do not resist the temptation to despair, we risk opening our hearts to negative forces, which sweep in and plunge the soul into bitterness, and even cynicism. (A simple test of our heart's condition is to see whether our spirit still kindles at the sight of others being blessed. If it does not, there is something seriously wrong.)

Hope is such a psychological necessity that, without it, the best of us are vulnerable to the scourges of fear and anxiety. Georges Bernanos, and other Catholic writers, claim that despair is the most insidious of all temptations. This is because the powers of darkness try hard to hide the fact that it is a temptation at all. How clever they are at making our despondency appear a natural response to the dilemmas that we face. How diligent they are in masking the ways in which God has led and blessed us in the past. How easily they shift our focus from the vision God has given to our own lamentable condition. How important it is to remember that we worship a God of hope, and that hope does not disappoint us![3]

Overcoming the Sense of Failure

As we have seen, behind Elijah's despair lay a crippling sense of failure. To feel that we have failed is one of the most disorientating of all emotions. Fear of failure stalks our nation, hinders creativity and pressurizes people into ways of living that are at a variance with all they really want to do. The man who has made no mistakes, however, has in all probability, made nothing worthwhile.

There is a sense in which the Lord can only truly use those who have come thoroughly to mistrust themselves. A Spanish proverb reminds us,

> 'He is always right who suspects that he makes mistakes.'

Oliver Cromwell put the same point yet more strongly when he said:

> 'I beseech you, in the bowels of Christ, to think it possible you may be mistaken!'

Such humility leads us away from despair, and into patterns of godly repentance. It also represents an important counter-balance to the more strident forms of triumphalism.

The Battle is the Lord's

Perhaps it is only those who have shared the same spiritual burdens as Elijah who can understand the weight of the dejection he felt at this time. Certain types of despondency are more difficult for the saint to bear than the sinner.

Whereas those whose hearts have been touched by the Lord feel acutely the pain of individuals, nations or churches which are going astray, the vain occupy and torment themselves with many matters of no consequence.[4]

We must be careful not to make glib judgements about those who have borne much greater strains than ourselves. As an old Red Indian proverb puts it,

> 'Help me never to judge another until I have walked for two weeks in his moccasins!'

Given the circumstances, it is easy to identify with Elijah's prayer. It is only fanatics, and the untested, who have never had to wrestle with a sense of their own dejection, as they measure the size of the task ahead with their pathetically inadequate resources. Nevertheless, it can never be a proper response, for it is tantamount to accepting Satan's assessment of the situation that we face. Surely the Lord, who had provided for His servant time and again in the past, could find a new way to do so now?

The battle is the Lord's, but we still need a heart for the fight. If there is one thing certain, it is that when we set out in faith to fulfil a mission for the Lord, there will always be a host of inner doubts to overcome, and people to tell us that we are attempting the impossible!

Again and again we will have to resist the pressure that fear places us under. Courage has nothing to do with not being afraid, but everything to do with being willing to go forward in spite of our fear. Courage is thus almost a contradiction in terms. It is, as G.K. Chesterton put it,

> 'a strong desire to live, taking the form of a readiness to die.'

Lord, fill us with Your courage, and help us to keep our eyes stayed on You!

Overcoming Giant Despair

There was a time when the entire Israelite army was reduced to paralysis by the sound of Goliath's challenge, and the size of the giant's shoulders. Similar temptations to despair afflict the Body of Christ today. Many of us will know what it is like to experience a particular 'giant' stepping forward every time we seek to take a step of faith. Listen to its deep and threatening taunts: 'You'll never be able to do that; you'll be left high and dry ... Who do you think you are?'

Fuelled by a low self-esteem, and reinforced by outward setbacks and disappointments, the temptation to despair becomes embedded in our minds, and tedious refrains endlessly torment us: 'If people knew what I was really like, they wouldn't love me ... God can't use me, I'm not even sure that He hears my prayers ...' These are immensely private battles, which must be fought and won.

It would have been tragic beyond words if the Lord had granted Elijah's impetuous request, and allowed him to perish in the desert in an unmarked grave. After all, much of his most far-reaching ministry still lay ahead of him – not to mention his friendship with Elisha, and all that came from that.

There will always be temptations to retreat from our calling. Satan is forever angling for us to yield to a sort of pact of non-aggression. His unstated offer ('I won't hurt you, if you won't hurt me') is designed to make us feel that the cost of our pilgrimage is too high – and hence to make us willing to settle for a less vigorous discipleship.

As always, our perspective is crucial. A tightrope walker fixes his gaze on some object far ahead to keep him steady. What he never does is to look down, or around. The Greek of Hebrews 12:2 provides the clue to overcoming Giant Despair when it speaks of *'looking away unto Jesus.'*

Our task is to respond with faith, and so disappoint

the devil's expectations. For while the negatively-minded see the potential for disaster in each difficulty that they face, the creatively courageous press in to see the Lord bring about new triumphs from the very same circumstances. Like a rose among thorns, fresh opportunities to prove the Lord's faithfulness lie hidden within every one of our dilemmas.

Mourning into Joy

It takes courage to keep trusting and praising the Lord when some longed-for door closes in our face. Not every legitimate hope that we harbour will come to fruition, or, at least, not immediately. Neither will we be spared the pain of having to contend with unexpected and painful disappointments along the way. Yet God can turn around for good even the attacks which men and Satan intended for evil – as we continue to trust Him.

How else can we interpret the shocking episode when Joseph's brothers decided to rid themselves of their boastful brother? Yet God used even this act of callous treachery in the long run to save the nation. Joseph was later able to recognise that it had been God, and not his brothers, who had delivered him to Egypt – and for the all important reason of preparing for the forthcoming famine.[5]

Is not this dramatic change of fortunes a foreshadowing of the greatest reversal of all time, when the finest man who has ever lived was put to death on a Cross? If God was able to turn the ultimate injustice round to be the final victory of all, is He not able to handle our relatively trifling setbacks?

Don't Give Up!

Could we but discern it, our temptations to despair are often little more than wounded vanity. We feel dejected less because we have hurt the Lord than because we have failed to live up to our mistakenly high standards of what we thought we could do (or be) for Him.

While it is right to have a deep horror of sin, it is better to have a still greater love of good. The Lord admires us more for having tried to do something for Him, and perhaps having failed in the attempt, than if we had attempted nothing through fear of getting it wrong.

That is not to say we will necessarily be spared all the consequences of our sins and stupidities. Many of us may still have to live with the after-effects of the rash things we have said or done. Yet we can take heart from the example of Elijah. There would still be much fruitful service ahead for him – just as there was for David after his lapse with Bathsheba.

God is merciful but not indulgent. The baby Bathsheba bore David died at birth. Had he been let off more lightly, the lesson would not have been scored deeply enough into his heart. As it was, the severity of his chastisement deterred him from ever again abusing his exalted position. But how futile it would have been if David had ended his days in endless remorse because of what he had done!

More people fail because they give up trying, than as the result of some actual failure. If we nurse a sense of guilt and failure, it not only makes it hard for us to accept God's loving forgiveness, it means we are effectively implying that our wretchedness is greater than His never-ending love!

As Selwyn Hughes puts it,

> 'The Lord Jesus is not against us for our sins, He is for us against our sins.'

It is dishonouring if we believe anything less. We are well on the way to being truly humble if we can repent of our stupidity, but still enjoy boundless confidence in God's forgiveness. Christ does not love us grudgingly, as if with gritted teeth. He is our Companion, who longs to show us the best path to follow. Every day is a fresh page that is waiting to be written – a brand new opportunity to live for the Lord. We never know what He is going to do next!

The Antidote to Despair

Winning battles of faith against despair not only brings to nought the gloomy predictions of Giant Despair, but also opens up whole new horizons for us. That does not mean that we may not lose some rounds on the way. Elijah himself had been fighting too many battles on too many fronts, and was, in consequence, physically and spiritually drained. Perhaps he was also suffering the haunting fear of being let down by God. His feelings can be summed up in one agonised question: 'What's the use of going on, Lord, if You're not with me?'

Superficially, Elijah's plight appears to resemble that of Jonah, who also sat down under a broom tree and wished aloud that he might die. But there the similarities between the two prophets end. Elijah fled when his life really was in danger, having completed the greater part of the work God had called him to do. By contrast, Jonah did his utmost to avoid even starting on his mission.

Moses once prayed in a time of great despair,

> *'If Your presence does not go up with us, do not send us up from here. How will anyone know that You are pleased with me and with Your people unless You go with us?'*

It was genuine anguish, not whingeing selfishness, that had made Moses cry out to God. Like Elijah, Moses had travailed too long in the heat of the day. Both had felt acutely that their mission was beyond their powers to accomplish. To Moses, God had shown Himself supremely merciful, giving him a wonderful promise:

> *'My Presence will go with you and I will give you rest.'*[6]

As hope rekindled in Moses' heart, he became still bolder, even going so far as to ask to be allowed to see the glory of God. This too the Lord permitted.[7]

Most people have heard of the Hebrew word *'ruach'* (the 'breath, wind or Spirit' of God). Fewer will be familiar with *'nu'ach'*, a verb that occurs on more than twenty occasions in the Bible. It means to rest or settle down, to be soothed or quieted; to be secure, to be still, and to dwell peacefully. God was promising to soothe and comfort His troubled servant with the restfulness of His presence. The Spirit of God delights to draw us closer to our heavenly homeland as we pray for His *'ruach'* to *'nuach'* (settle deeply) on us.

Elijah had been through a painful and protracted time of turmoil, and the Lord, in His kindness, granted Elijah a further period in the wilderness to help him recover from his intense ordeal. In Isaiah 28:12 the Lord presents His people with a wonderful offer:

> *'"This is the resting-place, let the weary rest"; and, "This is the place of repose."'*

The word used here, *'menuchah'*, is a derivative of *'nuach'*. It is the word used in Psalm 23:2: *'He leads me by the waters of "menuchah".'* It is a yet stronger exhortation to come to a place of quietness – and one we dare not refuse.

The Lord's Refreshing

When the battery of our camcorder runs out, it needs to be fully discharged, a stage known as 'refreshing'. Only when this process is complete does the actual process of recharging begin. There are parallels here in the way the Lord refreshes us beside still waters. At the end of the forty days, however, Elijah was 'discharged' rather than 'recharged'.

We find him curling up in a cave – a fitting place, one feels, for a man who had wanted to escape from everything and everyone.

For us, too, the Lord may permit all manner of obstacles to come our way before His work of refreshing is complete. When He resolves them all, in His own inimitable way, we are left with the joy of knowing that only the Lord could have brought about so great a victory.

We can be at peace, therefore, concerning our many present difficulties. The Lord will solve each one in its turn, provided we do not allow the terror of Jezebel to fill our minds, and quench our faith. We are so quick to assume the worst, and to suppose that the Lord has deserted us. The reality is quite different: our labour is far from being in vain.

We shall have more to say on overcoming despair in the chapter 'Confronted with God's Challenge'. In the meantime, the answer to our feelings of despair lies in what has been called 'The Sacrament of the Present'. If we can leave the past to God's infinite mercy, commit the present to His grace, and entrust the future to His boundless providence, there will be far fewer landing strips for discouragement. The more we give thanks to the Lord in all circumstances, the more we will experience His joy flooding in to refresh our soul.

Reflections

The Lord had asked Elijah a searching question: *'What are you doing here?'* The implication is clear: 'Why are you so far from your post?' The question may be a relevant one for us, too, when despair seizes hold of us. Let us spend a few moments with Him now and ask Him if there is anything the Lord would say to us concerning the way we handle our times of crisis.

Have we responded to our own difficulties with faith, or been dominated by our fears? Were we really called to be involved with that particular situation which so wore us out? Have we learnt to recognise the danger signals that indicate when our energy levels are depleted, and taken quality time off to compensate?

Selah

Lord, I recognise the devil's tactics for what they are – a desperate attempt to make me give up before Your victory comes. I acknowledge that my work would be unfulfilled were it to end right now, and I declare that You will yet fulfil all You have in mind for me to do.

Heal my hurts and confusions, increase my determination to trust You, and overcome my tendency to despair. I ask that the wind of Your *'Ruach'* (Spirit) may blow now through my life, to bring me to a deeper place of *'nu'ach'* (rest), so that I may serve You from a place of peace. In Jesus' Name, Amen.

References

1. Acts 4:19–20
2. Exodus 32:19; 1 Samuel 27:1
3. Romans 4:18, 5:5, 8:24–25, 15:13; Psalm 25:3–7ff
4. cf Paul's heart-longing for the Jews to be saved, and his daily concern for the well-being of the churches he had founded. See Romans 9:1–3; 2 Corinthians 11:28; Galatians 4:19–20.
5. Genesis 45:5; cf 50:20
6. Exodus 33:14–15. The word 'rest' comes from the Hebrew *'nu'ach'*.
7. Exodus 33:17, 21

Chapter 16

Angelic Restoration

'Then (Elijah) *lay down under the tree and fell asleep. All at once an angel touched him and said, "Get up and eat." He looked around, and there by his head was a cake of bread baked over hot coals, and a jar of water. He ate and drank and then lay down again.'* (1 Kings 19:5–6)

Elijah was in sore need of some special demonstration of God's love to re-equip him for the work ahead. The way in which the Lord restored His bruised and battered servant is one of the most beautiful illustrations in all Scripture of just how close the Shepherd is to us during our trials. What seemed to Elijah at the time to be the end of everything, would prove to be only the beginning of a new and glorious phase of service.

In retrospect, what the Lord did not say to Elijah is also striking. There was no 'last-chance' warning that he would be dismissed from the prophetic office unless he pulled his socks up; no point by point analysis of where he had gone wrong. What a wonderful reminder that at the heart of the universe lies the God who *'gives liberally to all, without reproach!'* [1]

At a time when they were in great need of encouragement, Jesus prepared breakfast for His disciples on the shores of Lake Galilee, cooking the meal over a charcoal fire.[2] This was a highly symbolic moment for one disciple in particular. It had been beside another charcoal fire that Peter had denied His Master. Now the Lord was recommissioning him for the work ahead.

For Elijah, the Lord began the healing process by giving him a deep sleep. What could be more precious? We can bear almost anything if we have had a good night's rest. Our understanding of God's love must never become so super-spiritual that we lose sight of practical realities. Then came food. An angel woke Elijah from his sleep, and there was a cake of bread cooking on a bed of hot coals, together with a jug of cool fresh water. This was better fare than the ravens had provided – this was the food of heaven!

The Role Angels Play

In a day when the work and activities of Satan and his demons (fallen angels) are so much in the news, it is all the more important to understand the role God's angels play. After all, their work is alluded to in over 350 verses in Scripture – far more than is accorded to the powers of darkness. May the Lord open our eyes to the realities of the spiritual world, and to the ministry of His unseen servants, even as He did for Elisha's servant.

From the moment of the Annunciation until His Resurrection, angels were the constant companions of the Lord Jesus. Had they not been with Him in the wilderness, He could not possibly have endured so gruelling an ordeal.[3] Neither would Elijah have survived now without their timely help.

As the climax of the ages draws near, we will see more clearly both the work of the evil one, and of God's resilient warriors, His angels. As the devil recognises how short his remaining time is, we will have increasing reason to be grateful for the constant watchfulness of the hosts of heaven.

It is unfortunate that many still associate angels with the winged creatures of fine art paintings – or with cherubic children taking part in kindergarten nativity plays. There is nothing childish about the ministry of God's messengers. Their power is so great that just one angel alone could slay the host of Sennacherib's army.[5]

As part of God's invisible creation, angels do not draw attention to themselves. This poses a problem for our rational materialistic generation – until, that is, we pause and remind ourselves of the limits of our sight and senses. Thinking people do not deny the existence of electricity or radio waves simply on the grounds that they have never seen them with the naked eye. Why, then, are we so full of arrogant assumptions when it comes to angels?

Because we neither see nor hear anything that looks like an angel, this does not mean that 'God's secret agents' are not hard at work on our behalf. The ministry of angels is far more extensive than most of us have understood. Occasionally, they take human form to accomplish some mission. It was not every day that Peter was allowed to see them, yet one appeared to him in prison, struck the shackles off his wrists, and led him out from an innermost cell into freedom.[4]

Where neither cafés nor hospitals exist, angels serve the children of God. Countless Christians can share Elijah's testimony concerning the help angels bring at times when they need it most. They aid us on our specific tasks, and help us enjoy a greater intimacy with the Lord Himself.

We see angels throughout Scripture on missions of both mercy and judgement. It was, for example, an angel who executed divine retribution on Herod for setting himself up as a god.[6] It is not that we should seek to devise a spiritual formula on 'how-to-escape-from-prisons-in-the-power-of-the-Spirit' – and neither should we develop the expectation that every jumped-up politician will meet so grisly an end! Building a doctrine out of an experience is never wise, but it is reassuring to remind ourselves of the power of these 'ministering spirits', who are sent to serve those who are honouring the Lord.[7]

Over the years I have come across many delightful stories of 'angels in disguise,' who turn up with some essential piece of advice or equipment just in the nick of time – before, quite literally, disappearing from sight. God uses angels to facilitate issues that would otherwise have remained unresolved, and to release people into God-anointed spheres of service.[8]

Angels are well known for the part they play in miracles of supply and support. What is needed will be provided, and what is damaged can be repaired. It would be the same in Elisha's ministry as it had been for Elijah – and God has not changed to this day.[9] Angels still reassure of God's love, meet people's needs, warn of God's impending judgement, and the imminent return of the Lord Jesus Christ, and then return to their place in the courts of the Lord.

Lessons from Exodus

In the wilderness, God sent His angel to prepare the way for His people. Since the appearance in Scripture of an angel is often tantamount to the presence of the Lord Himself, their words need to be taken seriously.[10]

> *'See, I am sending an angel ahead of you to guard you along the way and to bring you to the place I have prepared. Pay attention to him and listen to what he says. Do not rebel against him; he will not forgive your rebellion, since My Name is in him. If you listen carefully to what he says and do all that I say, I will be an enemy to your enemies and will oppose those who oppose you. My angel will go ahead of you and bring you into the land of the Amorites, Hittites, Perizzites, Canaanites, Hivites and Jebusites.'*[11]

We can learn much about the ministry of angels from this passage. First of all we discover something every child used to know, that these mighty beings are sent to guard the people of God. Just as an angel kept the Israelites safe from the pursuing Egyptian army before the crossing of the Red Sea, so they keep a constant watch over us.[12]

There are many accounts of hostile men being unable to attack a group of believers because of a shining presence of angelic beings around them. Interestingly, it has often transpired later on that Christians far away had felt an urgent call to pray for these people at the exact moment the angels appeared. This is a pointer to the important role that angels play in the whole realm of intercession. As we pray in agreement with each other, and at the leading of the Holy Spirit, angels are sent to assist the people and situations for which we are praying, often battling through intense opposition to bring their much needed help.[13]

Secondly, we can see that angels are involved in bringing us to the place God has prepared for us. It was an angel who told Philip to leave his revival campaign in Samaria and to go instead to the desert road that leads to Gaza.[14] It was there he met and converted a man who many believe to be the founder of the Church in Ethiopia.

We find something similar in the account of Cornelius, the Roman centurion.[15] The angel who appeared did not preach the gospel to him – God has entrusted that responsibility to men – but he did tell him how to get in touch with those who would. This angelic intervention proved to be God's way of leading not just one isolated centurion to salvation, but of enabling Gentiles everywhere to be incorporated into what had hitherto been exclusively Jewish congregations.

Thirdly, the Israelites were instructed to listen carefully to what the angel told them. When I first read this passage, I had some fairly hefty scruples to overcome. I thought that only God should be allowed to speak to us, and that to listen to angels might be downright dangerous. True, the prophet Zechariah seemed to enjoy conversations with them on something approaching a regular basis, but I was only too well aware of the devil's ability to disguise himself as an angel of light – and we are not Zechariah![16]

The Scriptures are clear, of course, that the Lord bestows His authority on angels to pass on His messages. The word *'angelos'*, in Greek, means a 'messenger'. When the angel revealed himself to another Zechariah (the father of John the Baptist) we can see this principle in operation.

> *'I am Gabriel. I stand in the presence of God, and I have been sent to speak to you and to tell you this good news.'*[17]

Sometimes when a deep stillness comes on us, unseen angels are helping us to worship God in spirit and in truth. A visiting speaker brought this word of prophecy at our very first prayer Conference:

> 'I am setting My people free in these days, and when you are one, I will do amazing things in your midst.'

On the recording we made, angels can be heard in the distance during the silence which followed the sharing of this word, their beautiful worship wonderfully confirming this powerful message.

Angels in History

Rather than focusing exclusively on God's mighty acts of deliverance in history, let me start by sharing from a family holiday a simple example of the practical help angels send. (You will probably be able to think of incidents in your own life along similar lines.) Walking through a wood one day, I discovered that I had lost the key to the cottage we were

staying in. As we retraced our footsteps along the path, I could see no sign of it. Rather than rummaging around in the undergrowth we had been walking through, I stopped and prayed with my daughter (then aged five) for an angel to show us where it was. As we made our way back, there was the key in the middle of the path! I am convinced it had not been there when we had looked the first time.

If we look more closely at (or rather behind) the pages of human history, we will find plenty of evidence concerning the involvement of angels. Daniel 10–11:1 affords us an example of the activity of angels in the wider affairs of mankind. In recent times, there is well-documented evidence concerning the appearance of a battalion of shining white figures who put a German army to flight at Mons, towards the end of the First World War.[18]

It has often been noted how the the Nazi High Command stopped sending their planes by day to bomb British airfields at the very moment when our last fighter reserves were in the air. What is even more remarkable is the role angels were seen to play in this combat. Air Chief Marshall Dowding is reputed to have commented that angels were seen on a number of occasions flying the planes after the pilots had been shot dead, continuing the battle that ultimately saved Europe from the Nazi tyranny.

The work of angels has been particularly noted in connection with the state of modern-day Israel. An angel was seen at the United Nations, guiding the hand of the Russian delegate who finally authorised Israel to become again its own nation. That Israel survived the initial wars at all against the surrounding Arab nations, despite being heavily outnumbered and outgunned, can only be considered, by any standards, an extraordinary miracle.

Equally as remarkable is what happened in 1973, when the combined onslaught of the Egyptian and Syrian armies caught the Israeli defences completely unprepared. (They were largely absent from their posts because they were commemorating Yom Kippur, the Day of Atonement.) A Syrian tank captain, poised to sweep over the virtually unmanned Israeli lines of defence, saw a hand stretched out from heaven. He found himself completely unable to advance. The Egyptian attack likewise ran inexplicably out of steam. Many believe that nothing short of the direct intervention of heaven prevented the nation of Israel from being overrun at that time.

More than ever, we need to know that we have a prayer-answering God. He still has the unlimited power of the host of heaven at His disposal, as the world plunges into the tumultuous events of the last days.

Who do Angels Help?

Angels are sent to help and protect not the proud and self-sufficient, but those who have a heart to honour the Lord.[19] The Israelites were warned, therefore, not to rebel against the angel, for Scripture reveals that angels are used as God's instruments of judgement.[20] It was an angel who destroyed the first-born of every family throughout Egypt on the night of the Passover, and an angel who declared the judgement of the Lord on a rebellious and unbelieving people at Bokim.[21] Again, at the end of the age, the reapers will be the angels.[22]

We do well to remember that God is, as the prophet Zechariah constantly refers to Him, *'The Lord of Hosts.'* He alone is in charge of human history – and the degree to which the host of heaven oversee the fine details of our lives is nothing short of amazing.

To commit ourselves to God is to prepare for adventure, and to be guided in ways we could never have foreseen. We must be open to all the workings of the Holy Spirit and not be afraid of unusual forms of help and guidance. But neither should we over-emphasize dreams, visions and angelic communications, lest we become like those who *'take their stand on visions, puffed up without reason by their sensuous minds.'*[23]

Perhaps in the light of all this, Elijah's reaction to the appearance of the angel is a shade disappointing. Elijah appears to look on the miraculous provision of the water and the food almost as if it was his by right. When we are under pressure, how easy it is to take all the Lord does for us for granted!

The angel came to Elijah twice. It is often only the second time the Lord sends us something that we really begin to appreciate its value. This special demonstration of God's care restored Elijah's faith, as well as his stomach. God may not have been promising to strike down Jezebel (which Elijah had doubtless been hoping for) but what He was doing was to initiate the process of setting His overwrought servant back on his feet.

There is a final delightful point to ponder as we consider the role of angels. Jesus told the Sadducees that we will one day be like the angels in heaven.[24] If this is to be our ultimate state in eternity, should we not begin to live like them now in the purity of our lifestyle? Angels are usually to be found either in an attitude of worship before the throne of God, or out and about on specific missions at the bidding of the Lord. May our lives reflect this balance, now drawing close to the Lord, and then going out on service for Him!

Reflections

When difficulties loom and human resources appear inadequate for the tasks and challenges that face us, it is an enormous comfort that we, like Elijah, are able to count on the unseen support of the heavenly host. It is good to remind ourselves that,

> *'The angel of the Lord encamps around those who fear Him.*[25]

Pause for a while to thank God for angelic deliverances, both in our own lives, and throughout human history. Write some of these down.

Selah

> Lord, help me to stand before Your presence in heavenly worship, and then to go out on specific missions for You. Guard and guide me with the protection of Your angels as I go about this work. In Jesus' name, Amen.

References

1. James 1:5
2. John 21:4–14
3. Mark 1:13
4. Acts 12:3–11, see also Acts 5:19, 27:23
5. Isaiah 37:36
6. Acts 12:23
7. Hebrews 1:14, 13:2; 2 Kings 19:35; cf Daniel 6:2; Genesis 19:15–16
8. Genesis 24:7, 40; cf Judges 6:11–23, cf 13:3ff
9. e.g. 2 Kings 4:42–44
10. e.g. Exodus 3:2–4; Joshua 5:13–6:5; cf Revelation 19:10
11. Exodus 23:20–23
12. Exodus 14:19–20; cf Matthew 18:10. The vicar of my previous church once stepped inadvertently off the pavement into the path of a double-decker bus. He loves to relate how he was literally picked up by the chest and placed back into safety!
13. Daniel 10:12
14. Acts 8:26
15. Acts 10:3–8
16. 2 Corinthians 11:14
17. Luke 1:19ff. Sadly, Zechariah did not believe the word spoken by the angel, and he was struck dumb until the joyous event came to pass (Luke 1:18–20, 61–64). The following texts also refer to the work of angels as messengers: Luke 1:26–38, 2:9–14; John 20:12; Matthew 28:5–7; cf Genesis 16:7ff, 31:11–13; Matthew 1:20, 24; 2:13, 19
18. This episode is quoted in a book called *Angels*, by Hope Price. Hope is a vicar's wife who has gathered dozens of such stories from around the world. It blessed me that this book was published by Pan, who are

not a specifically Christian publisher. These testimonies will therefore find their way into the hands of many who would not normally read Christian books.

19. Daniel 3:28, 6:22; Isaiah 37:36
20. Exodus 23:21–22
21. See Judges 2:1–5
22. Matthew 13:39, 16:27, 24:31, 25:31. It will be they who release great judgements on mankind (Revelation 8:7 onward).
23. Colossians 2:18
24. Matthew 12:25
25. Psalm 34:7

Chapter 17

Confronted with God's Challenge

'*So* (Elijah) *got up and ate and drank. Strengthened by that food, he travelled for forty days and forty nights until he reached Horeb, the mountain of God. There he went into a cave and spent the night.*

And the word of the Lord came to him: "What are you doing here, Elijah?" He replied, "I have been very zealous for the Lord God Almighty. The Israelites have rejected Your covenant, broken down Your altars, and put Your prophets to death with the sword. I am the only one left, and now they are trying to kill me too." The Lord said, "Go out and stand on the mountain in the presence of the Lord, for the Lord is about to pass by."'

(1 Kings 19:8–11)

God is looking for a people through whom He can be glorified. In Elijah He had found such a man, but even this 'giant of faith' needed to be reminded that it was not by might, nor by power, that he could bring about any lasting change in the country.

Unlike most of us, who become seriously off-balance if we stray too far from the body of Christ, Elijah, like all true prophets, had to obtain his reassurance directly from the Lord. The food God had provided gave him the strength to make the journey to Mount Horeb, where he would experience a fresh encounter with his Lord. This was no ordinary walk on the wild side. This was to be a forty-day pilgrimage to the mountain, and even, some say, to the very cave where God had revealed Himself to Moses.[1]

In those far-off days, no caravan tours wound their way through the desert to make Mount Horeb a shrine of pilgrimage. So far as we know, Elijah was the first visitor in centuries. There could be no place on earth more associated with the presence of God than Mount Horeb. This was where Moses had seen the burning bush, and had been given the Law after his epic sojourn alone with God.[2]

As he made his way through the wilderness, Moses must have constantly been in his mind. Had that great servant of the Lord ever been able to forgive himself his outburst of frustration, which had consigned the former prince to a forty year sojourn in the wilderness? Weaknesses exposed are not necessarily weaknesses overcome. It was to be another outburst of temper, forty years later, which deprived him forever of the chance of entering the Promised Land.[3]

Hope surged through Elijah as the holy mountain loomed before his eyes. Surely it would be here, where Moses had struck the rock that yielded a miraculous supply of water, and where he had lifted up his hands and prayed while Amalek was defeated, that God would draw close and deal once and for all with the menace Ahab and Jezebel posed to the nation?[4]

The Lord was longing to blow away the doubts and sorrows that had filled His servant's mind, but there were implications about the flight from Jezreel that Elijah still needed to face. That is why this most precious of encounters began, not with an embrace, but with a challenge. The Lord was determined to undo the damage striving was causing in Elijah's life.

After a night in a cave, the Lord met with His servant – but not at all in the way he might have hoped for. The encounter came in the form of a searching question: *'What are you doing here, Elijah?'* If Elijah had been looking for a pat on the head, and to be told that he was doing a wonderful job, then the Lord's question must have pierced him to the heart. What was he really doing here? Had he come all this way at God's leading – or merely because he was running away from Jezebel?

We may well imagine that it had taken Elijah the full forty days for the despair in his heart to ease. If the Lord waited so long to put this question, then it was because He knew that it was only now that Elijah was ready to hear it. The Lord holds back until we are strong enough to face such a challenge. The way in which Elijah parried the Lord's question (by insisting that he alone had been faithful) might seem to indicate that Elijah was in danger of making an idol out of his faithfulness.[5] Given the sorry state of the nation, and the traumas he had been through, it is hardly surprising that Elijah had persuaded himself that this was the case. He was mistaken, of course – just as we are whenever we begin to suppose that we are in any special.

An Encounter of Holiness

Rather than assuming that Elijah had become a touch complacent in his role as Prophet Number One, there is an altogether kinder way to interpret this episode. Elijah's heart-cry is strikingly similar to the despair Habakkuk would one day feel over the state of the nation. Like all true prophets, Elijah and Habakkuk spoke not only to the people on behalf of God, but to God on behalf of the people. Both shared a deep concern that the Lord did not appear to be doing anything. Both had to be shown that God was, in fact, doing a great deal.

Consider, too, those glorious moments when God met with Moses in the burning bush, and when Joshua encountered the leader of the Lord's armies immediately before his decisive battle against Jericho.[6] These mighty encounters took place in solitude, for God takes advantage of such times to make us face challenges we would otherwise run from.[7] Elijah discovered, like Moses and Joshua before him, not that God was on his side, but that he must be on His.

There is a type of Christianity that never progresses beyond rejoicing in being forgiven. Good though it is to celebrate, endless celebration can, paradoxically, become an excuse for not facing God's more searching challenges. Even our Christian service can then become a subtle form of evasion.

When God probed Elijah's motives, He found them sadly lacking. It is an unfortunate fact that our vices are more habit-forming than our virtues: they are easy to catch, but hard to break. No surprise, then, if the Lord has to use hammer and chisel to bring about that humility which enables us to inherit the kingdom of God!

There come times when the Lord puts His finger on actions and attitudes we might have been content to pass over in silence. We are pulled up short, not only for the things we have done, but equally for matters we have failed to attend to. Above all, the Lord convicts us of the lack of compassion and humility we have shown to virtually everyone we have been in contact with.

Just as wreckage that has long lain on the sea bed is exposed as the tide recedes, so these times of challenge expose wrong attitudes in our hearts. In a sense this is pure mercy. How will we know if we can face challenge with repentance, and loss with equanimity, unless we are put to the test?

In His loving wisdom, God has to puncture our self-delusions. He asks us questions that reveal the sins that lie half-buried in our self-centred hearts. It can be painful beyond words when these things are exposed. I, for one, usually find it easier to withstand purely external adversity, rather than to suffer in the full knowledge that it has come about through my own silly fault. Grandiose plans that are undergirded by insufficient humility come to a sticky end. Errors of judgement entail consequences which cannot always be avoided. But God is continually checking and monitoring our response, to see whether His chastisements are bringing about the necessary repentance in our hearts.

These are the critical junctures in our lives. The Lord sees the inherent pride that hinders many of us from being willing to retrace our steps, and that shrinks from having to accept the inevitable loss of face. Yet if we stubbornly try to hold on to the way things were, we risk losing all.

To realise that many of our motivations are depraved and distorted is a necessary stage in the process of sanctification. To dwell too long in this place of self-discovery, however, would be dangerous. We might find ourselves inadvertently agreeing with the Accuser of the Brethren that we really are worthless! Since we have a High Priest who sympathises with our weaknesses, we must be prepared to face our many failures and foibles – but then move on beyond them.

The ability to show mercy (to ourselves as well as towards others) is one of the fairest fruits of intimacy with God. If we pressurize ourselves, or others, into parroting platitudes of faith, the heart will remain unconvinced. Worse, it may become rebellious, and learn to perform for the approval of others. All this is far from the true freedom God has in mind for us.

It is comforting that even when we do fall into wildernesses of our own making, the Lord will still go out of His way to woo us back to the path of faith and duty. As the angel of the Lord found Hagar in the wilderness, so for Elijah too, there would be an encounter in the desert.[8]

A Burnt-out Burden-Bearer

Elijah's difficult task had been to plough up the hardened soil of a spiritually deceived generation, and make the people aware of the imminence of God's judgement. Perhaps he had secretly nursed unrealistic expectations that the leaders of the nation would convert immediately back to the God of their fathers in the aftermath of the victory on Mount Carmel. No sooner did his thoughts return to the grievous state of affairs in Israel, than a feeling of gloom settled on him again.

As we have seen, God did not reproach Elijah for this. True, He did point out that there were still seven thousand faithful souls in the land who had not bowed the knee to Baal, but even then He did not rub Elijah's nose in the fact. The Lord understands the peculiar pressures that burden-bearers face.

When a sensitive man or woman feels the pain of a hurting person, or society, but sees no way in which to discharge these feelings, it is hardly to be wondered at if they find themselves prone to illness, and susceptible to myriad addictions. Mind and body overload in the search for relief from a pain they are unable to express. Such people often go to great lengths to avoid confrontation, smoothing over issues that needed facing up to. Alternatively, they adopt a martyr's stance, heavily overlaid with self-pity. They become, in Loren Sandford's memorable words, 'peace-makers in the flesh.'

If we are not willing to share our inner hurts with those who are close to us, then we cause them to suffer doubly, not only because we have a problem, but also because we are not sharing it with them. If we do not know where the real issue lies, the chances are that our wife, husband or friend already has a pretty good idea!

To coin a proverb,

> 'Honesty can solve any problem, but touchiness repels.'

We might not be inclined to rank over-sensitivity as one of the greater sins, but how can you work with a devious or an

insecure person? It is exhausting! It is hard to love such people back to life, because as soon as you offer the slightest suggestion, no matter how lovingly, they retreat into their shell and begin to bristle. Lord, help us not to be so touchy!

Overcoming Satanic Strategies

The devil does not give in easily. Previously, he had been desperate to persuade Elijah that he had reached the end of the road. Now we find him adopting a new ploy. There are few more successful avenues for the powers of darkness to exploit than stirring up the bitter-sweet pangs of self-pity. Counterfeiting the tenderness of God, Satan would have been at pains to sympathise with Elijah. How awful that he, who had been so faithful to his God, should find himself so neglected now![9]

Neither do the powers of darkness normally have much difficulty in making us critical. We are quick to find fault with others, easily mistaking our prejudices for maturity. We need to watch our tongues. Just as we stressed earlier, regarding the matter of God's provision, how essential it is to avoid the 'but-what-if' syndrome, so we must also sound a warning against those endless 'buts' which gush from our mouths. We do it so automatically, qualifying our statements to the point where it sounds as though even our blessings are a problem! Worse, we add disclaimers to our simplest comments about people, all but ruining their reputation in their absence.

If criticism kills, then kind words, and appropriate actions, have the opposite effect. If we will seek the Lord, He will show us ways to love and serve those whom we are most tempted to criticise. After all, even if unjust accusations are coming our way, doesn't God know many worse things about us than we are actually being accused of?

If our love for the Lord, and His Body, the Church, has

become clouded with ambition, and our hearts filled with condescending and judgmental thoughts, it matters not that our mind teems with schemes and bright ideas. Our condition will not be helped by a diet of more blessings, for these might merely serve to confirm us in our deceitful contentment. Thus, those of us who claim to know so much about the Lord can still be riddled with pride, and many other wrong desires. We can be sure of this: we are in line for the challenge of the Lord!

Perfectionism: a Faulty Model

If some are eager to exercise power to satisfy their own desires, there are others (including many outwardly successful people) who are plagued by nagging feelings of inadequacy. Typically, these were children who grew up feeling they were not important, and that their parents had more important things to do than to be with them. Children who are praised flourish, whilst those who are constantly criticised and compared with others are easily crushed, unable to perform to the impossibly high standards expected of them.

Many apparently spiritual struggles aren't really spiritual at all, but come from damaging feelings of low self-esteem. Condemnation hovers around such people like the smog over Athens – until the grace of God chases it away.

A few timely words of encouragement can go a long way to spur us on.[10] What we must not do, of course, is to try to derive all our security from other people. If we have programmed ourselves to believe that we are not acceptable, it is too much for any human person to convince us of the opposite. Better by far to 'forgive' God for making us the way that we are, than to expect unrealistic things from each other. Otherwise we will find ourselves withdrawing from people and becoming increasingly isolated and alienated.

If we find ourselves beginning to wonder whether the Lord could not have arranged this or that detail better on our behalf, we are embarking on a slippery slope. Once we mistrust His plan, we soon begin to entertain doubts about the Planner Himself.

It is a flawed theology to say, 'Well, I know God loves me, but I just can't live with myself.' We must be careful. We are speaking against someone whom God has cared for lovingly, provided for abundantly, and planned for perfectly. Is that honouring? Or fair?

For most of us, it is not a sudden experience that will right this imbalance, so much as a daily living out of the truth of God's Word. To a large extent, how happy we will be depends on the depths of our gratitude, and the state of our inner thought life.

> *'For as a man thinketh in his heart, so he is.'*[11]

This is not a position we will necessarily reach easily. We often spiritualize the process of self-belittling that goes on so laboriously in our mind, and give it some suitably pious name such as 'The work of Sanctification', or 'Self-crucifixion'. It would often be nearer the truth to accept it is just a lack of basic trust.

It is hard to worship a God who, as we perceive it, is never satisfied with us. Inward guilt makes us feel we must always try hard to be acceptable – but we fear in our heart that we never will be. A sense of divine disapproval hovers over us, which, inevitably, we transmit to others. Even if we preach all the doctrine right, something comes across in our manner as being not quite right.

Perfectionism is a counterfeit of intimacy with God, because it makes us focus more on what we feel we 'ought' to be doing, instead of getting on with what we actually can do. It deceives us into supposing that if only we were to do this or that, then God will accept us, and everything will fall into place. It is a striving after the wind.

The worst thing about perfectionism is the anger that lies just below the surface. Apparently holy (or placid) people finally rebel against the 'oughts' they feel God has imposed on them, and resent their failure to be the kind of person they thought they ought to be. Such anger is not objective reality of course; it is directed against the caricature of a disapproving God their own perfectionism has concocted.

God is passionately concerned about justice, but perfectionists become obsessed with it. We must learn to face this anger, and so come free of its pernicious influence. Otherwise we fall into denial, denying that we are angry, because 'a good Christian would never lose his temper.'

Perfectionists are hard to live with, because the model they are following is a faulty one. You can normally recognise those who are caught up in it by their violent mood swings. These are disconcerting precisely because you never know what to expect when you meet them. If these less readily acknowledged sins are not faced, our children risk growing up subconsciously believing that God is as unpredictable, irrational and unreliable as we have been.

The desire to be a 'Super-Christian' dies hard, and perfectionists become easily dispirited through apparent failures. The truth is that some issues we care about deeply will not resolve in the way that we had hoped. Even Paul and Barnabas 'agreed to disagree', and found themselves unable to work together for a season.

Sometimes we may have to battle against the dark cloud of depression. Most Christians have little understanding about depression, partly, perhaps, because they suppose it is something no true believer ought to suffer from. It is easy to assume that we are doing well if we do not happen to suffer from it ourselves – but this may be more a reflection on our temperament and constitution than any real indication of our spiritual maturity. The Psalms are much more realistic about our times of despair than most Christians are – and they have been a great comfort for sufferers through the centuries.

The first thing to stress is that depression does not always root back to a specific sin. It may have a lot more to do with our personality structure, emotional history or simple body chemistry. Neither is it necessarily a sign of spiritual failure. Sometimes, as for Elijah, it is 'kickback' following some great spiritual success.

Since it is the grace of God which puts an end to the perfectionist's perpetual sense of guilt, let us pray for the Lord to set us free from the cancer of perfectionism, so that we can enter in and enjoy His grace. His tailor-made yoke will suit both our personality and our particular calling.

God loves to achieve great things through weak people – so let us give Him the opportunity to do so! William Carey, the first Protestant missionary to India, wrote,

> 'Expect great things from God, and attempt great things for God.'

Why deny the gifts the Lord has given us? Why go back on the vision He has given us? Don't let the desires that God has placed within us be wrecked by Satan's propaganda machine. Jam his wavelengths, believe the opposite, and refuse all fears and doubts!

David Seamans suggests that we should ask God to check us every time we begin to belittle ourselves.[12] Since this process may occur far more often than we realise, it will take serious resolve to put this exercise into practice. It will involve learning to receive the utterly undeserved, but freely given, grace of the Lord.

Reflections

In the course of the average day, over 12,000 thoughts pass through our mind. I wish more of mine were of any eternal value! It is well worthwhile examining the subjects (and the objects) to which our imagination returns again and again. Do they glorify the Lord, or do they merely lead to insatiable cravings, which reduce our capacity to be open to the promptings of the Holy Spirit? Amy Carmichael wrote,

> 'Beware what you set your heart on, for it shall be yours.'

Are not so many of our words likewise designed merely to impress others?

Pray and meditate on these words of the Psalmist:

> *'Set a guard over my mouth, O Lord;*
> *keep watch over the door of my lips.*
> *Let not my heart be drawn to what is evil.'*[13]

Listen, too, to the heartfelt appeal of the writer of the book of Ecclesiasticus.[14]

> *'O for a sentry to guard my mouth, and a seal of discretion to close my lips, to keep them from being my downfall, and to keep my tongue from causing my ruin! Lord, Father and Ruler of my life, do not abandon me to the tongue's control, or allow me to fall down on its account. O for wisdom's lash to curb my thoughts and to discipline my mind, without overlooking my mistakes or condoning my sins! ... Many people have been killed by the sword, but not so many as by the tongue.'*

Selah

Thank You, Father, for being so long-suffering with us. Lord, we welcome Your challenge. Forgive us when we mistrust You, and lash out at people who would do us good. Forgive us that we are so intolerant, and so quick to defend ourselves. Show us those attitudes which need to change – and grant us strength to overcome them. Help us to speak words that build people up, and which release Your blessing. In Jesus' name, Amen.

References

1. Exodus 33:22
2. This too had lasted forty days and nights. See Exodus 3:1–4; Deuteronomy 4:15
3. Deuteronomy 1:37
4. cf Exodus 3:12, 19:3
5. Elijah must have held this belief strongly, because he repeats it on no fewer than three separate occasions: 1 Kings 18:22, 19:10, 14
6. Exodus 3:2–4; Joshua 5:13–15; cf Isaiah 6
7. e.g. Genesis 32:24–28
8. Genesis 16:13
9. Hannah Hurnard's marvellous allegory of the Christian life, *Hind's Feet on High Places* (Kingsway Publications) graphically illustrates this process. Foremost among the enemies Much Afraid meets as she makes her pilgrimage to the high places is Self-Pity. We would heartily commend this book.
10. Hebrews 10:24
11. Proverbs 23:7 (KJV)
12. David Seamans, *Healing Damaged Emotions* (Scripture Press Foundation).
13. Psalm 141:3–4
14. Sirach 22:27–23:2, 28:18; cf James 3:6–11. The book of Ecclesiasticus, or Sirach, is included in Catholic versions of the Bible.

Chapter 18

Symbols of His Power

'Then a great and powerful wind tore the mountains apart and shattered the rocks before the Lord, but the Lord was not in the wind. After the wind there was an earthquake, but the Lord was not in the earthquake. After the earthquake came a fire, but the Lord was not in the fire. And after the fire came a gentle whisper. When Elijah heard it, he pulled his cloak over his face and went out and stood at the mouth of the cave.

Then a voice said to him, "What are you doing here, Elijah?" He replied, "I have been very zealous for the Lord God Almighty. The Israelites have rejected Your covenant, broken down Your altars, and put Your prophets to death with the sword. I am the only one left, and now they are trying to kill me too."'

(1 Kings 19:11b–14)

I love the way God handles His servant. Elijah pours out his anger and his frustration, and God goes out of His way to reassure him that He is still with him. There is no hint of reproach, just a necessary reminder that His ways are higher than ours. As He dealt with Jacob, David and Jeremiah at times when their faith faltered, so He gently set Elijah free from the delusion that everything depended on him. What a God!

The Lord had promised to pass close by, and Elijah prepared himself for the wonderful moment when he would again feel God's familiar presence with him. First, however, he would be treated to an impressive display of the power of God. From the entrance of his cave, Elijah watched the awesome violence of a storm rushing through the deep granite gorges.

What could be a more fitting way for God to reveal Himself? Had He not spoken to Job out of a whirlwind, and would He not appear to Ezekiel in a great windstorm?[1] Jeremiah compared God's judgement to a whirling storm that sweeps everything before it. Nahum even proclaimed that His way is in the whirlwind and storm.[2]

It must have been a terrifying spectacle. Huge chunks of granite were tossed into the air as they crashed down the mountainside. There is an irresistible strength in the wind of God, which neither the work of men nor creation itself can withstand. We can imagine Elijah in those days before storm-proof anoraks, huddled in his cave, wishing he had a fire to shelter by.

It is no coincidence that the work of the Spirit is likened to a wind.[3] What is the move of the Spirit that is blowing through so many parts of the Church except the breath of God? In our own day we have witnessed an awesome wind of holiness sweeping through both Church and nation, exposing sin and shaking complacency. The hurricane that swept through the south of England in 1987, and the shaking that occurred on the Stock Exchange at the same time, were crucial reminders of heaven's right, and power, to overthrow all the pride of man's hopes and achievements.

Unlike most of us, however, Elijah was already familiar with the God of the whirlwind. Powerful though this wind was, the Lord had nothing new to teach his storm-tossed warrior through it. Suddenly, there came something still more frightening: an earthquake. It is a terrifying sensation when the earth, the symbol of our stability, ceases to support us. Whole cities can be laid to waste within minutes of such shaking.

An earthquake is caused by huge tectonic plates grinding against each other. The Bible adds to this natural understanding the supernatural interpretation that it may also be a sign of the heavenly powers impacting the Earth.

Consider, for example, the earthquakes that accompanied the giving of the Law at Mount Sinai, or the tremor that marked the Israelites defeat of the Philistines. The earthquake which swallowed Korah and his friends, when they rebelled against Moses, and the still larger one in Amos's day are other prime examples of God's judgement on a rebellious people.[4]

With such powerful precedents, we are hardly surprised to discover that a mighty earthquake accompanied the death of the Lord Jesus on the Cross. Later, the building the disciples were meeting in would be shaken in answer to their intense prayers. Yet another earthquake set Paul and Silas free from their unjust imprisonment, and led to the conversion of their jailer.[5] More recent quakes in Romania and Armenia have likewise paved the way for great spiritual harvests in their aftermath.

When London was struck by two such quakes in the late eighteenth century, they were taken by the Church as a serious warning and as a call to repentance. It is a sad reflection that we in the West no longer heed the Power behind earthquakes. But Scripture predicts that there are still many mighty earthquakes ahead.[6]

Considering all the upheavals he had already been through, however, Elijah felt as though God was saying nothing new to him through the earthquake. Then came a terrible fire. Again, we need to remember the setting: sun-scorched scrubland, where huge fires can be started by a single flash of lightning.

God is revealed throughout Scripture as the One who answers out of fire. Since fire is also considered the sign that a sacrifice has been accepted, Elijah must have expected to see God revealed in it. The crash of the thunder overhead, the howling of the wind, the quaking of the earth and the crackling of the flames must have overwhelmed the prophet's senses, even as they sharpened his anticipation.

With each fresh manifestation of Nature's might, Elijah must have looked to see the power and vengeance of God unleashed against the apostate nation. Hurricanes, earthquakes and firestorms seemed entirely appropriate symbols to indicate the judgement of God.[7] Much though the flames may have reminded him of the great triumph on Mount Carmel, however, God had nothing fresh to show him through them. Elijah had already endured more than one baptism of fire, as the Lord burnt up the dross in his life.

The Still Small Voice

The Lord came to Elijah, not by works of violence, but in a new and deeper way. One translator renders this delightfully as being 'with the sound of silence.' It is a phrase pregnant with awe and mystery. After all the elemental cacophony, stillness reigned again at last.

Elijah pulled his cloak over his face and rushed to the edge of the cave to meet with his God. Here at last was the presence he had grown to know and love so well during those prolonged days by the brook Cherith, before the mighty winds and storms had swept through his life. Perhaps his joy was mixed with awe and self-abasement, for there is nothing that makes us so aware of the holiness of God as when His presence draws near to us. We are humbled when He speaks, and chastened by the memory of our own unfaithfulness.

It was as though God were saying,

> 'You thought that because things did not turn out the way you expected, I had not been working. You are

completely mistaken. I am simply working in a different way. I know the things that Jezebel has done, but I want you to know that I am still in control.'

Elijah was amazed and overwhelmed, but he was still unable to grasp the meaning of all that he had seen and heard. In a retort of self-justification, he could only repeat the refrain he had programmed himself to believe.[8]

Slowly, the still small voice breathed peace into the tumult of his soul. The German word for breast feeding (*'stillen'*) beautifully evokes the mother quieting the child by her presence and her breast milk. It is a perfect picture of how the Lord meets our deepest needs.

Love is Stronger than Force

The work God had begun in Elijah so many years ago was now complete. God was restoring him to a calling he had at times wanted to run away from – and what prophet or pastor has not felt tempted to do the same at one time or another? God was about to recommission Elijah for active service, and to entrust him with some of the most important undertakings of his life. Now he would have to retrace his steps, resume his work and embrace new challenges. These, in turn, would prepare the way for a major dynastic change in the Middle East, and for a yet greater work of the Spirit in Israel.

What had Elijah learnt by fleeing to the desert? That it was not for him to remove himself from the ministry to which God had entrusted him! Perhaps, too, that God's gentler ways are often His best. Love is stronger than force, and the gentleness of God's mercy can accomplish more than the wind of His power. So often, His coming is not dramatic at all, but so gentle that it is easily missed.

He comes like the dew to refresh us, and His Spirit as a dove.

To live for God's glory does not mean that we have to scale the heights of spectacular contests on Mount Carmel, or do extraordinary things, before we become acceptable to Him. As someone put it,

> 'He has not saved us to be a sensation, but to be a servant.'

God esteems faithfulness and devotion. The steady influence of a quiet consistent life bears far more fruit than we generally realize.

Reflections

1. In what ways can we trace the work of the wind of holiness in our Church and society?
2. Ponder the 'earthquakes' that have shaken our own life and disturbed our complacency. What has been their outcome?
3. Consider the baptism of fire that John promised the Lord Jesus would send. How has this affected our life?
4. In what ways have we experienced the Still Small Voice?

Selah

> Thank You Lord that You are in the winds that blow, the fires that burn up the dross, and even in the earthquakes that so unsettle us. Most of all we thank You that You want us to abide in You, and to discern the quieter accents of Your love. Continue to develop this ability in each one of us, that we may be both intimate with You, and effective for You. In Jesus' name, Amen.

References

1. Job 38:1, 40:6; Ezekiel 1:4
2. Jeremiah 23:9, 25:32, 30:23; Nahum 1:3
3. John 3:8
4. Exodus 19:18; 1 Samuel 14:15; Numbers 16:31–33; Amos 1:1
5. Matthew 27:51–54; Acts 4:31, 16:25ff
6. e.g. Revelation 11:13, 16:15–21; cf Isaiah 29:6; Joel 2:10; Zechariah 14:4–5
7. cf Isaiah 13:13, 29:6, 24:19–20; Luke 3:16–17
8. See 1 Kings 19:13–14

Chapter 19

The Dark Speech of God

'The Lord said to him ... "Elisha will put to death any who escape the sword of Jehu."' (1 Kings 19:15–17)

It gives the Father great joy to communicate with His children. One word from God can release so much blessing! Elijah could never have survived the drought, let alone the hostility of Ahab and Jezebel, had the Lord not told him step by step what to do. The still small voice that so refreshed Elijah in the cave reminds us of the importance of these brief, but far-reaching, encounters the Lord granted His servant. They reassured him of His presence, challenged his faith and imparted fresh direction and authority.

Many of the words the Lord spoke to Elijah were clear and simple commands. Others were more complicated in their outworking. Elisha, for instance, would not put anyone to death himself. The word was a true one, but the details require unravelling.

If we examine the way the Lord Jesus speaks in the New Testament, or indeed in our own lives, we will find that much of what He says is elliptical, and requires further clarification.

'Jesus spoke the word to them, as much as they could understand. He did not say anything to them without

> *using a parable. But when He was alone with His own disciples, He explained everything.'*[1]

Sometimes we strive too hard to find a literal interpretation for a word or picture, when the Lord is simply showing us a type or an example. You could say that Paul's vision of the Macedonian man calling to him across the water turned out to be Lydia! The images in the Book of Revelation, likewise, are symbols capable of many different interpretations.

From time to time, God changes His way of communicating with us. Had the disciples continued to look for Jesus to appear to them in bodily form after the Ascension, they would have been disappointed. It was not that the door of heaven had swung shut on them, but simply that the Holy Spirit intended to communicate the will of the Lord Jesus to them from then on by new methods.

Understanding Dark Speech

In their perceptive book *The Elijah Task*, John and Paula Sandford go into some detail regarding what they term 'dark speech': these less direct ways in which God speaks to us. At its simplest, 'dark speech' occurs when we think God is saying one thing to us, only to find out later that He was actually speaking about something rather different.

A parable talks about one subject (such as fish, or a lost sheep) but its real meaning lies elsewhere. Clearly, we need the key if we are to understand this type of teaching. Unlike the disciples, who were privileged to have 'face to face' understanding of the secrets of the Kingdom, Jesus taught the crowds almost exclusively by means of parables. They were both a helpful teaching aid and a fulfilment of the Messianic prophecy,

> *'I will open My mouth in a parable; I will utter dark sayings from of old.'*[2]

Long ago, in the golden age of Greek philosophy, Socrates realized that people learn more by finding things out for themselves than by being told what to do. He developed a technique of asking people questions in such a way as to make them see the truth of a situation for themselves. This kind of teaching has been known as 'Socratic' ever since.

Jewish teaching traditions ran along similar lines. The Lord Jesus helped His disciples to come to a deeper understanding of who He was more by pointers, parables and analogies than by direct proclamation. His memorable illustrations stimulated the imaginations of His hearers, and prompted them to reason and understand for themselves.

The gift of tongues is another example of dark speech. We build ourselves up in the Lord by using it, but we may have no idea what mysteries we are proclaiming, or praying for. What is only partially clear on earth has its full realisation in heaven.[3] Now we see dimly, as in a mirror; then we shall see face to face.[4]

The way we look at images in a mirror reverses our normal perspective. We see the right on the left and the left on the right, but we quickly learn to interpret the images the right way round. Similarly, the Hebrew word translated 'dark speech' or 'dark saying' (*'chidah'*) literally means a 'knot'. It is a particularly appropriate expression since we often have to unravel what God is saying to us.

At a major cross-roads in his life, a man heard the Lord say to him, 'Probation'. Concluding that the Lord was calling him to the Probation Service, he applied for a training course. Before taking up the post, the Lord directed him to check the word 'probation' in his dictionary. When he discovered that the word could also refer to a 'time of testing in a religious context', he realised that God had tested his willingness, but actually had other plans in mind for him. In due time, the Lord opened the way for him to become the leader of a thriving church.

I can recall many occasions when I felt the Lord telling me to go and visit someone, only to find that they were out. Because I was on the move, however, I was in the right place to meet someone else – which was what God had intended all along. In retrospect it is clear why we were led as we were, but it can be puzzling at the time. God prompts us into one course of action, and then takes over by His sovereign initiative.

Dark Speech Develops Dependency

Why does God use dark speech? Perhaps it is because, if we knew too much in advance, and could always be sure of hearing clearly, pride would puff us up (or fear would fill our hearts). We would be in great danger of abusing our knowledge by trying to make events work out in our own strength. Therefore the Lord uses dark speech to keep us dependent. He speaks as much, or as little, as He needs to, and then looks for a response of faith and obedience.

Similarly, He does not always rebuke us openly, but allows circumstances to work out in such a way as to bring us first to a clearer understanding of a situation, and then, as needs be, to a deeper repentance.

In the whole realm of listening to God there will inevitably be times of disappointment and confusion, when we mishear, or misinterpret what we thought we had heard from God. Perhaps it has to be this way. If our hearing were more accurate, people would come to rely on us rather than learn to listen to God for themselves. The miracle is that He manages to overcome our sinful self-centredness to be able to speak to us at all.

John and Paula Sandford remind us pertinently that nobody graduates in the school of listening with their pride intact! If we hold back on trying to listen because we have made mistakes in the past, we are no wiser than the person who vows never to get into a car again after being involved in a car accident.

When Paul declared that he had been prevented from being able to cross over into Macedonia, he made it clear that this was not through any lack of prayerfulness concerning the decision in the first place.[5] Unlike so many of us, he refused to allow unexpected setbacks and changes of plan to diminish his trust in the Lord.

True, we do well to examine our mistakes carefully, to see if there are areas where we are particularly susceptible to error. Misjudgements in the past may be a pointer to some 'structural' weakness. Providing there is no fundamental deception in our hearts, however, God will always make sure that enough of our hearing is right in order to fulfil His purposes.

Reflections

Try and recall occasions when you have felt the Lord leading you in one direction, only to discover later that He had something quite different in mind. What does this have to teach us about His sovereignty – and our need for step-by-step obedience?

Selah

> Lord, help us to recognise Your leadings, and to trust what You are saying to us. Grant us courage first to listen, and then to act on what You show us. Thank You that You grant us help as and when we need it. In Jesus' name, Amen.

References

1. Mark 4:33–34
2. Psalm 78:2. This expression 'dark sayings' occurs elsewhere in the Scriptures:

'A wise man hears and will increase learning, and a man of understanding shall attain unto wise counsels; to understand a proverb and the interpretation; the words of the wise and their dark sayings.'
(Proverbs 1:5–6 KJV; cf Psalm 49:3–4)

3. 1 Corinthians 14:41, 13:9–12
4. cf Job 19:26–27; 1 John 3:2; Revelation 22:4. The word 'dimly', as the RSV translates 1 Corinthians 13:12, literally means 'in a riddle', or 'in an enigma'. This ties in well with the reference to riddles in Numbers 12:8.
5. 2 Corinthians 1:16–17

Chapter 20

The Judgements of God

'The Lord said to Elijah, "Go back the way you came, and go to the Desert of Damascus. When you get there, anoint Hazael king over Aram. Also, anoint Jehu son of Nimshi king over Israel, and anoint Elisha son of Shaphat from Abel Meholah to succeed you as prophet. Jehu will put to death any who escape the sword of Hazael, and Elisha will put to death any who escape the sword of Jehu. Yet I reserve seven thousand in Israel – all whose knees have not bowed down to Baal, and all whose mouths have not kissed him."'

(1 Kings 19:15–18)

The people of Israel may have renounced Baal worship, but their hearts were still hard. Three years of drought had neither weaned them from their backslidings nor turned them to the Lord. We can discern a wealth of hidden meaning, therefore, behind the Lord's commission to appoint Hazael and Jehu to be the next monarchs of their nations.

First, Elijah was told to appoint Hazael to be the next king of the powerful Aramean (Syrian) nation. Here was a man who would stoop to anything in order to fulfil his ambitions, and who would one day launch an invasion against Israel. Secondly, Elijah was sent to proclaim Jehu, a rough and ready army man, to be the next king of Israel, with the express purpose of overthrowing the house of Ahab. Elijah's final commission was to appoint a young farmer as his own successor.

For a man who had so recently believed himself to be indispensable for the task of delivering Israel from its apostasy, this last command must have been particularly welcome. Elijah had repeatedly lamented that he alone was faithful in the land, and here was God, raising up the perfect companion for him. Whereas Saul hounded David, as a potential rival, at the point of his spear, Elijah would do everything he could to develop Elisha's ministry. The contrast between Elijah's nurturing spirit, and King Saul's insane jealousy, could hardly be greater.

It is always God's way that others should take our place, and go further than we ourselves have done. Any church leadership that is failing to plan ahead to raise up its successors is lacking in its vision, for the Lord is always thinking of the next generation.

The Judgement of God

It is important for us to try to understand why such motley people as Jehu and Hazael were needed to complete God's dealings with His rebellious people. The fact that God was prepared to appoint them at all is a reminder that His purposes stretch far beyond the walls of Church or Temple.

Earlier, we made a comparison between Elijah and Habakkuk. It is a curious coincidence that in both generations, God's plan involved the raising up of unscrupulous men to be the scourge of His people. By choosing Hazael to be king over Aram, God was declaring that His time had come for the dynasty of Benhadad. Since Hazael would shortly invade Israel, it is hard to interpret this appointment in any other light than as a judgement on apostate Israel.[1] Jehu may have served to rid the land of the worst excesses of Baal worship, but he can hardly be considered a paradigm of righteousness.

This theme of judgement is never far from the Elijah narrative. What is important to realise is that this is not some obscure Old Testament concept. The judgements of God are everywhere in the Bible – but all too little attention is given to the subject in most churches today.[2]

Those who uncompromisingly proclaim the wrath of God, unrelieved by a proper appreciation of His mercy and long-suffering, tend to display all the winsomness of a chunk of granite! For lack of a proper understanding of this theme, however, many Christians know all too little of the fear of God in their lives. So it is that some churches have wandered off into mere sentimentality, while others have become doctrine-bound through fear of embracing error. Both extremes are a distortion.

We find the perfect balance in the Person of the Lord Jesus Himself, who came into the world full of grace and truth.[3] Had He come only with grace, history might perhaps remember Him as little more than a laissez-faire do-gooder, effectively preaching a 'Do-what-you-please-if-it-makes-you-feel-good' message. Nothing could be further from the Jesus we meet in the gospels. Equally, were He to treat us purely as we deserve according to His absolute holiness, then which of us would not be crushed by the weight of our sinfulness?

We need experience no confusion in reconciling the God of Love with the One who was, and is, the Judge of the World. He is, and always has been, the God of all mercy, but when unconfessed sin encounters the holiness and zeal of the Lord, then shaking and judgement are inevitable.

The Wrath of God

This is where our study of the life of Elijah bears so heavily on our own condition today. We too are part of a society that has turned to embrace whichever pleasures, fancies or gods most appeal to us. Are we too not ripe for judgement? In Billy Graham's words,

> 'If God spares the nations of the West, He will have to apologise to Sodom and Gomorrah!'

God is angry when the Church pronounces arbitrarily on issues He has already declared to be absolutes, and when we fail to make a clear distinction between right and wrong. The modern habit of ridiculing certainty, and elevating doubt, is not glorifying. Scripture is full of warnings that, where there is insufficient repentance, the Lord Jesus will *'come and fight against us with the sword of His mouth.'*[4] There is a real danger that God will hide His face from us, and allow more and more disasters to be visited on us.[5]

One reason why so many fail to heed these warnings is because they have been taught to dismiss all talk of God's wrath. It is neither 'politically correct', nor does it fit in with people's picture of how they would like God to be. Moreover, we tend to associate wrath with destructive emotions. After all, we usually regret it when we lose our tempers! But human anger is neither a full nor an accurate picture of the wrath of God.

Scripture teaches so plainly about the wrath of God that we simply cannot afford to heed the siren songs of those who claim there is no anger in His heart.[6] The love of God contains and embraces wrath, for holiness has but one standard: the righteousness of the Lord Jesus Christ. Why should we be surprised if 'the God of justice' reveals His justice? Just because He does not send His bills in every week, people do not get away with breaking God's laws. Ultimately, it is probably less true to say that people break God's laws than that they break us. Truth is a strong support of the righteous, but it is a hammer that destroys falsehood.[7] When evil has reached its full flowering, the judgement of God falls – and usually in such a way as to justify God's intervention in everybody's eyes.[8]

Those who 'major' on a God of love presumably derive their understanding from their reading of the gospels. In which case they need to take into account the full picture the gospels present us with. It is a patchy and selective reading which embraces His love whilst ignoring His holiness. It leads to nothing but a gospel of our own making.[9]

Sharing the Lord's Heart

At the very time when the principalities and powers of darkness are gathering themselves for the final battle for the heart and mind of mankind, large parts of the Church have been rendered ineffective in the struggle against a strong secular challenge. It is heartbreaking to watch God having to expose the unbelief and the immorality that lie hidden in the heart of the Church. Although we see these things, most of us still do not make the connection, and realise that this too is part of the judgement of God. It is astonishing how blind we can be.

God's will does not consist of a set of inflexible doctrines. Rather it embraces and considers our response. Thus Brother Andrew writes that while 'God's nature and character are eternal and unchanging, His plans are flexible.' To a large extent they are dependent on our repentance, and our intercession.

Although much of the Church remains taken up with its own concerns, I believe it gives the Lord great pleasure when we are prepared to give Him the undivided love of our hearts. But He grieves when we set aside the call for repentance and righteousness in favour of the outwardly more exciting, never realising that this in turn will become predictable as the years go by. The heart of God burns with zeal to bless those who seek Him earnestly – but it is red-hot against all such things which affront Him.

Mercy Triumphs Over Judgement

Studying this inglorious period of Israel's history is no mere academic exercise: it contains a sobering warning, as well as spiritual solutions, for our own generation. It is only by facing the challenge of God that we will ever become one with the God of Mercy. We will need to comfort and steady ourselves with this truth at times when so many parts of the world are exploding in violence, famine and warfare, leaving people hurt, bewildered and confused.

God had already pronounced His sentence on backslidden Israel, just as He has against our society today. We are not speaking here merely of some future event; a process of shaking is taking place right now across almost every area of our national life. Did we really expect a holy God to be content merely to watch impassively while Church leaders mislead the people concerning His very nature? True, the Lord prefers to reform than to remove – the outworkings of judgement are grievous to God Himself – but He will not hold back when it is necessary.[10]

The Lord has revealed His judgement against us: our task is therefore to accept His assessment of the situation, and to cry out to Him for mercy. Time and opportunity are always offered for repentance, for it is ever the longing of the Lord to restore and to revive.[11]

Less optimistically, we must also recognize that people find it easier to blame circumstances than to face up to their own shortcomings. The book of Revelation warns that this will be the case right up until the end of human history. Even though God sends disaster after disaster in order to attract our attention, many will prefer to curse God rather than repent.[12]

Whereas Nineveh responded to the message of repentance and so was saved, many other societies have fared less well.[13] Where mercy is not sought, then God will allow us to be overtaken by the things on which we have so foolishly set our hearts.

In and through the shaking, God is training a prophetic people, who will cultivate the minutes to pray for God's presence to return in power to the spiritual wastelands which the western nations have become. All that God does is for cleansing and purification. When men and nations reach the end of their own resources, they are far more likely to turn to the living God, who can transform any situation.[14]

The Lord is looking for two things: to save the lost, and to find a people who will worship Him in Spirit and in Truth. He is restoring gifts and ministries to His Church, and causing her to shine with increasing vigour and in far greater beauty. This is no time for doing things which have no eternal value, and which bring Him no glory. He is refining us so that we can go and do as Jesus did, and help hurting people to experience the transforming power of God, and so enjoy the fruits of mercy.

Reflections

Ponder the thought that *'mercy triumphs over judgement.'*[15]
In what ways have you seen God's judgement at work?[16]
What criteria would you suggest to help distinguish between God's judgement (on a person, church or nation) and His 'normal' discipline?[17]

Selah

> *'Oh, that You would rend the heavens and come down, that the mountains would tremble before You! As when fire sets twigs ablaze and causes water to boil, come down to make Your name known to Your enemies, and cause the nations to quake before You! For when You did awesome things that we did not expect, You came down,*

and the mountains trembled before You. Since ancient times no-one has heard, no ear has perceived, no eye has seen any God besides You, who acts on behalf of those who wait for Him.' (Isaiah 64:1–4)

Sovereign Lord, You used Elijah so powerfully to show forth Your judgements in the world. Help us to understand Your ways better, so that we can both pray and act in tune with Your heart. We cry to You to forgive our foolish ways and our backsliding as a nation. We cry to You for mercy. We have tried to bring revival to our land, and we have done no more than scratch the surface of the nation. Only You can bring this power – and You long to do so. We plead with You to come, and to do whatever is necessary in our own lives to help bring this about. In Jesus' name, Amen.

References

1. 2 Kings 10:31. In a sense, one could say that sending Elijah to the widow in Zarephath, rather than to someone in Israel, was in itself a judgement on the nation for its refusal to welcome the prophet God had sent them. See Luke 4:24–27.
2. e.g. Deuteronomy 32:20ff; Romans 1:24–32; cf Ezekiel 10:18–11:13
3. John 1:14
4. Revelation 2:16; see also 2:5
5. See and study Deuteronomy 32:15–43
6. cf Hebrews 12:5–12; Revelation 2:19
7. Jeremiah 23:29
8. Paradoxically, it could be argued that the judgements of God sometimes seem to fall on the righteous rather than on the unrighteous. Thus Jesus was put to death while His tormentors lived on. There is much to ponder in Isaiah 57:1:

   'The righteous perish, and no-one ponders it in his heart; devout men are taken away, and no-one understands that the righteous are taken away to be spared from evil.'

9. 2 Timothy 4:3–4; cf Revelation 2:6, 21–23
10. cf Isaiah 28:21, 27:8–9, 31:2; Romans 11:20–23

11. Jeremiah 3:12–13, 19–22, 4:1–2; Isaiah 30:18; cf Lamentations 3:28–29, 48–50, 2:18–19
12. Revelation 16:9
13. Jonah 3:8–10; cf Jeremiah 25:30–32; Genesis 15:16; Revelation chapters 6, 8–9, 15–16, 18–19
14. Deuteronomy 32:36
15. James 2:13
16. Unlike any previous generation, many believers today find it hard to grasp the concept of the wrath of God. The following provide a number of 'starter' texts to help introduce us to the concept. Numbers 16:45–48; Deuteronomy 1:32–38, 9:13–19; 2 Chronicles 28:8–15; Isaiah 47:5–11, 54:8–9, 57:16–21, 64:9–12; Lamentations 4:12–13, 5:21–22; Matthew 3:7; 1 Thessalonians 1:10, 5:9; Romans 2:1–8, 12:17–21; Revelation 6:16; Matthew 23; cf Zechariah 11:17; Ezekiel 34:1–6; Micah 2:6–3:12; James 5:1–6; Amos 5:5, 6:1, 4
17. If you are struggling to know where to begin with this very searching issue, try thinking of men in the Bible who fell under God's judgement. What were the key reasons why mercy was not shown to them? Study the word 'judgement' every time it appears in the New Testament. Compare and contrast that with the Old Testament, for example, as in the book of Psalms or Jeremiah. On a rather different level, try meditating on the word 'judgement' as it is used in the book of Proverbs in its wider meaning of 'good sense'.

Chapter 21

When My People are One

'So Elijah went ... and found Elisha son of Shaphat ... Then he set out to follow Elijah and became his attendant.' (1 Kings 19:19, 21)

The young man was ploughing quietly in his field, driving the hindmost of twelve pairs of oxen. Looking up he saw a man waving to him, his cloak billowing out behind him as he strode across the field towards him. Something about the way he walked seemed strangely familiar. Surely not – his eyes must be deceiving him! It looked just like the prophet Elijah, whom he had seen so recently on Mount Carmel, confounding the prophets of Baal. Whatever could he be doing here?

Without a single word of greeting, Elijah came up to him and threw his cloak over him. Elisha understood all that was implied by that gesture. Elijah's cloak was the symbol of his authority in the prophetic office, and his mind reeled at the implications. Whatever the reasoning behind Elijah's unexpected visit, he, out of all the young men in Israel, was being called to become Elijah's apprentice and ultimate successor.

An Authentic Leader

As we have studied Elijah's lonely struggles, have we not longed for him to be blessed with a worthy friend and companion? Obadiah may not have been suitable, but God delights to bring together those who will bless and refresh each other. Here indeed was one of the 7,000 who had never bowed the knee to Baal, a man ideally suited to share life with God's chosen prophet.

The call of Elisha is strikingly similar to that of the first disciples. For him, too, there was a clear choice that had to be made, a willingness to break with all that was settled and certain in his life. Those who respond to such an invitation discover that God has the very best in mind for them.

Elijah's response to Elisha's request to be allowed to return home to kiss his parents goodbye is ambiguous. *'Go back,'* Elijah replied. *'What have I done to you?'*[1] On the one hand, it is as though Elijah is saying, 'Of course you can go back home. What claim do I have on your life?' These would be the wise words of any leader, who wanted people to make decisions for themselves, and to avoid them becoming too dependent on them.

On the other hand, Elijah may well have wanted to impress on Elisha what an honour it was to have been called to the prophetic office. It was extremely important, therefore, that he did not forget what had just taken place. From now on, Elisha's life would be governed by a completely new set of priorities.

It is a sign of Elisha's rightness of spirit that he allowed nothing to hold him back. Like David himself, he was being called from the fields into the service of the living God, and everyone must know the news. As a sign that he had reached a decisive cross-roads, he broke his yokes, and turned them into fire wood. Then he slaughtered the oxen, and served them as food for his friends and family: a freewill sacrifice of momentous significance.

Elijah was, in every way, a trustworthy model for the prophet-in-training. We might have expected a man entrusted with so difficult a mission to have become aloof and unapproachable, driving others even as he drove himself. Elijah may at times appear austere (especially when compared with Elisha) but he had shown himself a gracious guest in the home in Zarephath. Now he was to spend the best part of a decade with his young apprentice.

Elisha was destined to exercise a ministry that lasted twice as long as Elijah's, and which would glorify the Lord by performing perhaps twice as many miracles. Yet Elisha would have had no ministry but for Elijah's faithful obedience through the long desert years. Moreover, he would benefit from an advantage that had been denied to Elijah himself, learning his craft at the side of one who was already moving in the power of the Spirit.

I can think of a host of reasons why I prefer to say, 'Follow Jesus, not me!' Yet Paul did not hesitate to say, *'Join with others in imitating my example.'*[2] We learn so much just by being alongside godly men and women. Something of their faith and anointing – as well as their graciousness and wisdom – rubs off on us. We are blessed if we have fathers and mothers in Christ who will nurture, train and care for us. We are equally blessed if we are prepared to serve in such a capacity ourselves.

Two Are Better Than One

All who have enjoyed fruitful friendships or a happy marriage would whole-heartedly agree that,

> *'Two are better than one because they have a good return for their work; if one falls down, his friend can help him up. Though one may be overpowered, two can defend themselves. A cord of three strands is not quickly broken.'*[3]

The mystery of these verses lies in the unexpected reference to the cord of three strands. It is a pointer to the glorious truth that when two or more are gathered in His name, the Lord Jesus Himself is present in our midst.

Milton was right when he wrote:

> 'Loneliness is the first thing which God's eye named not good.'

Apart from the friendship of God, what can bless us more than the care and affection of good friends? Was not Jonathan's friendship a mainstay in David's life? Did not Timothy's love support and revitalise Paul? To develop and maintain friendships that refresh our spirits, and bear fruit for the Lord, repays the effort involved a thousand times over.[4]

The friendship that flowered and flourished between Elijah and Elisha was to have enormous implications for the nation. In God's economy, one plus one equals far more than two.[5] It is the strength of the ties that bind us together which will determine how fruitful we will be in carrying forward the work of Christ.

Where there is friendship, and effective discipleship, there we will find honest counsel and heartfelt prayer. Where there is no such trust, we may be inclined to pray self-consciously and to act in secret. When the companions of the Lord give their hearts to one another, there is no limit to the creative initiatives the Lord can lead us into.

The success of our task as a Church depends on us being a united people. In the chapter 'Angelic Restoration', I referred to a prophetic word which a visiting speaker brought at one of our conferences. It has become deeply etched in my understanding of what God is doing among His people:

> 'I am setting My people free in these days; and when you are one, I will do great wonders in your midst.'

It is when we are together in heart and spirit that God moves among us in the fullness of His power. Yet we also know that much of Church life is soured by petty jealousies and outright hostilities. By far the biggest problem missionaries face is not the food or culture, but the sheer difficulty of getting along together.

The reasons for this may lie far beyond mere awkwardness of personality. Demonic spirits of division are ever on the prowl to target key leaders, in the hope of causing damaging splits within the body of Christ. We need to keep our guard up, for these powers are skilled at exploiting our particular weaknesses. It was in just such a way that they entered Judas Iscariot. We must recognise suspicion, resentment and mistrust for what they are, and renounce them quickly.

Together Together

On the day of Pentecost, when the Church was born in such power, the disciples were *'all together in one place.'*[6] The Greek text makes the same point twice. They were 'together together'; in other words, together in heart as well as in the same building.

We can derive deep meaning from the twelve stones that Elijah gathered together to form an altar on Mount Carmel. Just as the Lord saw the nation of Israel as one, so He views His Church as one, despite its many splinterings and schisms.

There is no place for narrow sectarianism. It is easy to talk of unity, when all we often mean by it is that others should agree with us. It is powerful if we are able to bless and honour those whom God has raised up, even if we personally do not happen to agree with them on every point. If we cannot own God's workmanship in their lives, is it fair to expect others to recognise it in us?

Arrogance soon has a way of turning into outright division. The moment we assume our perspective to be the best and only one, we leave ourselves stranded on our hilltop, flying our little banner:

> 'There's only thee and me left – and I've got serious reservations about thee!'

Will those who love the Lord wholeheartedly serve Him as one man, and so fulfil the Lord Jesus' heart-felt prayer that we may be one? Is it just a comforting cliché to speak of God's people as being one? Let me put the question another way round: to what extent are we prepared to heed the impassioned scriptural exhortations to be one?

> *'I appeal to you brothers, in the name of our Lord Jesus Christ, that there may be no divisions among you, and that you may be perfectly united in mind and thought ... I plead with Euodia and I plead with Syntyche to agree with each other in the Lord.'*[7]

True doctrinal soundness is crucial for the well-being of the Church, yet we are not called to refuse fellowship with those who express their faith in somewhat different ways from ourselves.[8] Differences in the body of Christ are rarely sinful – but arguing over them can be. As George MacDonald put it,

> 'It is not by driving away our brother that we can be alone with God.'

We are doing the enemy's work for him when we pick endless fault with those who have been washed and cleansed by the blood of Jesus.

It is only when we focus our attention on Jesus Himself, our one true Shepherd, that we move in harmony with all who have a real love for the Lord.[9] A man called Salik once wrote,

> 'When the rams are looking at the Shepherd, their woolly coats rub up against each other companionably;

but when they look at each other they see only horns!'

The more we are seeking to encourage and pray for each other's ministries, the less chance there is of relationships breaking down. We will also waste less time comparing ourselves with each other. Such comparisons can only ever lead to pride, if we think that we are better than others, or to despondency, if we feel inferior.[10]

Instead of trying to apportion ourselves our place in 'Fame's Hall of Honour', as C.S. Lewis so eloquently put it, the heart must relearn its first lesson, that it is loved and accepted by the grace of God. What cause can there be for bragging, since every anointed ministry has been given for the benefit of the whole Church, and is but the Lord's gift anyway?[11]

Satan's kingdom cannot stand against a united, praying people who constantly affirm their love both for the Lord and for each other.[12] The Psalmist urges us to shout for joy when we see others faring well.[13] Here is the perfect antidote to competitive jealousy. We are to rejoice when others go further and faster in life, and with the Lord, than we do.

Since by grace we belong to the Lord's worldwide Church, we are to think globally, but act locally. Each fellowship throughout the world, like every tribe and nation, is a jewel in the Lord's crown, each making its own special contribution. It is especially good for us to spend time praying for His richest blessing on people, churches and ministries we do not normally associate with.

Reflections

Pray and ponder the example of Elijah setting out to disciple Elisha. Who has most effectively discipled you? How did they do it? Then consider: how faithful a friend are you to others? Are there particular people the Lord would have you befriend and nurture?

Samuel Johnson wrote:

> 'If a man does not make new acquaintances as he advances through life, he will soon find himself left alone. A man should keep his friendships in constant repair.'

Finally, take Paul's eulogy of love in 1 Corinthians 13, and substitute 'Am I' instead of 'Love is'. For example, 'Am I patient and kind? Do I envy or boast? Am I proud, or rude, self-seeking or easily angered? Do I keep a record of wrongs? Do I always protect, always trust, always hope, always persevere?'[14]

Selah

> Father, we can never thank You enough for all the friends that You have given us. Especially for those who have affirmed and nurtured us, and cared enough to challenge and correct us. Make us sensitive to guide and guard each other's hearts. I pray that You will harness our friendships to accomplish many good things for Your Kingdom. I wait on You now to see if there is anything that You would have us do together, or if any are in special need...
>
> Join me in spirit to the people You would have me come alongside. Send Elijahs into my life to disciple me, and Elishas whom I may disciple.
>
> I pray that You will lift the veil that stops my non-believing friends and family from seeing You as You really are. Reach their hearts with Your saving grace and let them see the light of Christ.
>
> Help me to build bridges between Your people. I open my heart to my Christian brothers and sisters

across the world, and pray for the work of Your Church to go forward. In Jesus' name, Amen.

References

1. 1 Kings 19:20
2. 1 Corinthians 4:16
3. Ecclesiastes 4:9–12
4. Proverbs 18:24, 27:17
5. cf Romans 14:7–13; 1 Corinthians 12:12–31; 1 John 4:20–21
6. Acts 2:1
7. 1 Corinthians 1:10; Philippians 4:2; cf 2:1–5
8. cf Romans 14:2–4
9. Ephesians 4:2–6, 11–13
10. cf 2 Corinthians 10:12; Galatians 6:4
11. 1 Corinthians 4:7
12. Matthew 23:8; cf Ephesians 6:18
13. Psalm 20:5
14. 1 Corinthians 13:3–7

Chapter 22

A Heart of Mourning

'Elisha stared at Hazael with a fixed gaze until he felt ashamed. Then the man of God began to weep.'[1]

(2 Kings 8:11)

Looking beyond Elijah's lifetime, we find Elisha continuing his prophetic mission, both in guiding the leaders of the nation, and in decreeing the judgements of heaven on kings and nations alike. Thus, when Benhadad, the king of Aram fell ill, he sent Hazael to consult the Lord through Elisha as to whether or not he would recover. The Lord showed Elisha that Benhadad's illness was not, of itself, fatal – but that Hazael would take advantage of it to kill the king and seize the throne for himself. To Elisha's deep distress he also foresaw how cruelly Hazael would persecute the Israelites.[2]

Like all true prophets, Elijah and Elisha were allowed into the courts of the Lord to hear the thoughts and decrees of heaven. God shares with His friends not only the joys of heaven, but also His sadnesses. Developing an 'Elijah heart' means allowing the things which grieve God to touch our hearts.

It is not as simple as it sounds, to find a spiritual way of expressing our concern. The sheer amount of evil and suffering we are surrounded by can easily crush our spirit. But if our awareness of these evils does not lead us to mourn, we are likely to do no more than to fear – or to moan.

As we encounter unspiritual practices in the Church, and tragedies in the world, we will often experience the Lord's grief and anger. In the book of Jeremiah, the Lord's lament centred on the fact that the false prophets had not stood in the council of the Lord to understand His will.[3] Like Paul, we must be willing to suffer in spirit for the Church,

> '*...I fill up in my flesh what is still lacking in Christ's afflictions, for the sake of His body, which is the Church.*'[4]

When judgement fell in Ezekiel's day, God sovereignly spared those who grieved over the detestable sins of those around them. This is not melancholia. We can mourn in prayer, precisely because we are secure in the love of God.

Over a period of time, our hearts become filled with repentance because we have not made Him Lord of our lives, and Lord of our land. God hears the prayers of those who care. He uses our repentance to avert, or at least to mitigate, the severity of His judgement on our land.[5]

The Prayer of Identification

In a good novel it is easy to identify with the characters as we see them interacting in varying situations. They become so much a part of our lives that we may even come to regard them as having a 'real' life outside the pages of their book. How much more, then, should we be able to identify with the people we are called to pray for!

It is the nature of God to be one with those on whom He has set His love.[6] Just as Jesus fully identified with mankind by dwelling among us as a man, so today, as the Christmas hymn puts it,

> 'He feeleth for our sadness and He shareth in our gladness.'

There can be no greater pain than that of love which is refused and rejected. Something of this anguish was made clear to us one day, when Rosalind and I saw the Lord on the cross in a vision. We were together with Him looking out over the city of Jerusalem. Although we could neither see nor hear the mocking crowds, what affected us most was the sense of utter desolation and loneliness. The very people He had come to save had nailed Him to the cross, and He was unable to reach out and help them, because they had refused to respond to His love. In one sense, it is as though the Lord is still on the cross because, as a nation, we have refused to let Him accomplish His saving work in our lives.

The Lord mourns because so few are prepared to share their hearts and lives with Him. If Jesus wept over Jerusalem's rejection of Him, how can we not weep too for our uncaring world? Real prayer, as we have seen, is born of the same compassion which moved the Lord Jesus to

> *'offer up prayers and petitions with loud cries and tears.'*[7]

Jesus said that we are blessed when we mourn.[8] Intense times of such mourning can come on us at completely unexpected moments. We may be travelling, or walking around a town, when the Spirit stirs within us, and we find ourselves pouring out our hearts in prayer, as we see the emptiness in people's lives.

At a time when so many of God's children are suffering around the world for their faith, and struggling to make ends meet, God is giving us a chance to lighten their oppression by sharing in it spiritually.[9] As we meet in the joy of His presence, and in the freedom He has given us as a nation, it is good to remember those who are suffering for the sake of righteousness. It is selfish if we do not.

From Head to Heart

Part of the fruit of being close to the Lord is that prayer enables us to be close to people far away. As members of one body, what is happening to our brothers and sisters in Africa, China, and other parts of the world should be of immediate concern to us. It is important to take the trouble to find out what is going on, so that we can pray informedly for God's mercy to triumph over the powers of darkness.

Imagination is helpful in all types of prayer. Those who are oppressed or imprisoned for their faith, for example, need more than just physical strength: they need our prayers to hold fast to the faith, and to be spared agonies of anxiety at being separated from their loved ones.

For nearly three years I tried to pray for a man in a concentration camp. But I often forgot him, and allowed the distance between us to be a hindrance to my faith. When I saw a photograph of him on his release, and heard his testimony of how God had kept and blessed him during those long years of imprisonment, I was ashamed at how unfaithful I had been in supporting him.

Brother Andrew relates how he was praying with a local group for Christians who were being persecuted. News was suddenly brought to them that a young girl, who they all knew personally, had been taken seriously ill. The prayer meeting changed gear immediately, as everybody poured their hearts out for their friend. The Lord restored the girl, but He used the episode to illustrate how easy it is for our prayers to become perfunctory when we have no first-hand involvement in a situation. May the Lord make His burdens real in our heart!

'Liquid' Prayer

Judgement is shown in the Bible to be according to opportunity. The Lord Jesus wept over Jerusalem because it had failed to acknowledge the hour of its visitation.[10] Already He could see in His spirit the terrible disasters that would come on the city some forty years later when it was so cruelly sacked by the Roman army.

Jesus grieved, likewise, over the cities in which so many of His miracles had been performed. He warned that it would be worse for Bethsaida and Capernaum than for the pagan towns of Sodom and Gomorrah, precisely because these places had never been exposed to the Truth.[11]

There are, at the end of the day, only two kinds of nations – those that say 'It can't happen here,' and those which say, 'We thought it couldn't happen here.' The history of the world consists largely of empires that have been raised up, only to collapse under the weight of their own sinfulness. This, again, is why we in the West have so much to repent of. Our prolonged exposure to the light of the gospel makes our complacency inexcusable.[12]

But how we are to respond? Biographies of prayer warriors alternately inspire us with the vision of what our prayer life could be like – and discourage us because they are so far removed from our own experience. Our spirits stir (but our flesh quails!) when we read of Jeremiah, who so longed for his people to return to God that he cried out,

> *'O that my head were a spring of water, my eyes a fountain of tears.'*[13]

It is the same when we hear of John Knox kneeling in the snow, to plead for God's mercy to fall on his beloved Scotland, and a host of other mighty men and women of faith.

The matter boils down to how seriously we desire to see God move. The more wholehearted we are in our prayers, the more we will see the power of God released. The Jewish rabbis regarded tears as the highest form of prayer. Spurgeon described tears as 'liquid prayer'. When Luke records that

Jesus prayed 'more earnestly' in the Garden of Gethsemane, the English translation barely hints at the intensity of the real meaning of the Greek word, which might more accurately be translated: 'with greater stretched-outedness'.[14]

The devil dampens our willingness to pray by playing on our fear of suffering. He is, after all, the author of so much of it. I believe that almost everyone who has suffered for the Lord once doubted whether they would be able to remain faithful to Him during times of pressure.

A story which has helped many to come to terms with the prospect of suffering concerns the young Corrie Ten Boom. At the age of four she had a great fear of dying, and she asked her father what it would be like. That saintly man, who later met a brutal death at the hands of the Nazis, asked her another question by way of a reply: 'When we go to Amsterdam, when do I buy the ticket?' 'Just before we get on the train, of course,' she answered him. 'Then in just the same way,' her father went on, 'God will give us grace when we need it – not in advance!'

In later years, Corrie was to prove the truth of these words. Sent to Ravensbruck concentration camp for sheltering Jewish families, she experienced all the horrors which the perverted Nazi regime was capable of devising. She was finally released – by a clerical error! – on the day before all women of her age were put to death. Corrie toured the world for a further forty years, proclaiming wherever she went that there is no pit so deep that Jesus is not deeper still. The tears shed in Ravensbruck released a harvest all around the world.

Sharing the Lord's Heart

In a Roman penal colony on the island of Patmos, whence he had been exiled for his faith, an angel gave John a scroll to eat. It tasted as sweet as honey in his mouth, but it turned his stomach sour.

Ezekiel had had a similar experience, centuries before.[15] John and Ezekiel both discovered that eating the scroll was the outward sign of an inward call to take a hard message to a people who did not want to hear it. But the Lord did not leave Ezekiel and John to struggle on their own. He is merciful to those He calls to embrace such a message, and draws them deep into the glorious intimacy of His presence.[16]

God has a scroll prepared for us, too, which is at once sweet but bitter. I remember one night lying awake, feeling acutely God's grief concerning the violent events of the Crystal Night, which marked the start of the Nazi atrocities against the Jewish people. For the Lord the pain of that terrible pre-war night was as though it were yesterday.

Some five months before hostilities broke out, I felt a great sense of grief, as the Lord showed me the many Iraqis who would lose their lives in the Gulf War, destroyed through Sadaam Hussein's stubborn intransigence. On another occasion, at one of our prayer conferences, we were praying for children who had been abused. We experienced a strong sense of the Lord's grief and anger over all that had happened. One of the group was given an exquisitely moving lament, promising that to those who seek His face, He will reveal His heart: tears as well as joy.

Yes, He is the God of joy and gladness, but He is also a God of mourning, who wants us to share in all of His heart. Do not be afraid to let Him mould and shape your heart to share His pain and suffering. He will lead you gently, never asking more of you than He knows that you can bear. But where are the intercessors? Where are those who are willing to learn to mourn with Him?

Some years ago, a group of us were praying in the New Year. It was one of those frustrating evenings, when it felt for all the world as though our prayers were hitting the roof and coming straight back down again. One of us was even given a picture of a drum-skin stretched tight across the ceiling. When we asked the Lord what was wrong, He showed us that it was our lack of honesty with each other which was holding His Spirit back.

Repentance proved the key to a fuller flow of the Spirit. (It so often does!) 'From heaviness to heavenlyness,' we became aware of the Lord's close presence, and found ourselves worshipping in a completely new dimension, until finally one girl was left singing a beautiful melody that she was hearing in the courts of heaven.

Out of this most intimate time of prayer the Lord spoke to us:

> 'It is not for your sakes alone that you come into My courts in this way, My children, but for Mine. For when you worship Me in holiness, then is My power released in your land.'

The Lord hears the prayers that come from the heart, and He responds to them in power. Our tears are precious to Him. As we seek His face, we will find ourselves reaching out in love for many aspects of our national life. Is it too much to hope that we will find the mercy of the Cross drawing close, *'until the day dawns and the morning star rises in our hearts?'*[17]

Reflections

Do we mourn in prayer over things we know to be wrong? Or do we merely moan about them?

Selah

> Lord, make my heart as soft as Yours, so that I can share more of Your heart. Let me feel as You do, even when You mourn, so that You can release Your power

through my prayers. I pray this for the extension of Your kingdom. In Jesus' name, Amen.

References

1. Read 2 Kings 8:7–15
2. cf 1 Samuel 15:11; Exodus 32; Ezekiel 8:6; Revelation chapters 2–3. It is not that the Lord despairs over the state of the world – but He does grieve over it.
3. Jeremiah 18:22; cf 23:18. How can our compassion not be mixed with grief and anger when we pray for our land? The Church's task, in speaking to the nation with a clear prophetic voice, has been made infinitely harder by the faltering voices which deride sound doctrine and undermine biblical wisdom.
4. Colossians 1:24; cf Ezekiel 4:4–17. Our Lord was grieved at the hardness of heart of the Scribes and Pharisees, who refused to repent when they witnessed the miracles of the kingdom. These men not only excluded themselves from the purpose of God for their generation, but hindered others from discovering it, too, and so brought double judgement on themselves.
5. Jeremiah 5:1, 12:11; cf Ezekiel 9:3–6
6. John 17:20–24; Luke 22:31–32
7. Luke 19:41; cf Matthew 23:37; Hebrews 5:7
8. Matthew 5:4
9. cf Hebrews 13:3
10. Luke 19:41–44; cf 13:44
11. Matthew 11:20–24
12. cf Amos 3:2–3; Ezekiel 16:49. The nature of this sinfulness revolves around its self-centredness – and a corresponding unwillingness to reach out to share what God has given with others. I believe this is a key reason why our own nation is in such peril.
13. Jeremiah 9:1
14. Luke 22:44
15. Ezekiel 2:9–3:5
16. Ezekiel 1:26–28; cf Revelation chapters 1 and 4
17. 2 Peter 1:19

Chapter 23

The Prophetic Ministry

'Then the word of the Lord came to Elijah the Tishbite: "Go down to meet Ahab, king of Israel, who rules in Samaria. He is now in Naboth's vineyard, where he has gone to take possession of it. Say to him, 'This is what the Lord says: "Have you not murdered a man and seized his property?"'" ...

Ahab said to Elijah, "So you have found me, my enemy!" "I have found you," he answered, "because you have sold yourself to do evil in the eyes of the Lord. I am going to bring disaster on you. I will consume your descendants and cut off from Ahab every last male in Israel."

...(There was never a man like Ahab, who sold himself to do evil in the eyes of the Lord, urged on by Jezebel his wife. He behaved in the vilest manner by going after idols, like the Amorites the Lord drove out before Israel.) When Ahab heard these words, he tore his clothes, put on sackcloth and fasted. He lay in sackcloth and went around meekly.' (See 1 Kings 21:17–29)

Six years have passed since the mighty confrontation on Mount Carmel. The Lord had been merciful to Israel during the intervening years. He had raised up other prophets, and brought about a mighty deliverance from the vastly superior army of Ben-Hadad of Syria.[1] One thing had not changed, however, and that was the underlying condition of Ahab's heart. Once again he had failed in his duty, this time by sparing an adversary whom God had determined to depose. In a symbolic gesture, that was strikingly reminiscent of Nathan's challenge to David, a courageous young prophet rebuked the king to his face. Never one to willingly accept the warnings God sent, Ahab returned to his palace in Samaria 'sullen and angry.'[2]

Considering the weight of Ahab's sinfulness, it is little short of amazing that God continued to persevere with such a ruler. But that is the way the Lord is. So long as there is any hope left that a man may repent, the Hound of Heaven continues to woo and to warn. But there is a limit.

The Final Straw

Ahab had set his heart on possessing a little garden that adjoined his property. He offered Naboth, his neighbour, a better vineyard elsewhere. It never occurred to him that Naboth would decline his request to buy the land, because it contravened the law of God.[3] Naboth was quite within his right to turn down Ahab's advances – but the king and queen of Israel did not see it that way. Outraged at seeing her husband rebuffed, the queen devised a vile stratagem to secure the property. Feigning a religious fast, she used the law of God, which she despised so intensely, to forward her own wicked purposes. Jezebel arranged for false witnesses to come forward to condemn the unfortunate Naboth on the charge of having cursed both God and king.

When a nation allows people like Jezebel to reign, there are many innocent victims like Naboth. Evil rulers lead weaker people astray, and cause the nation to lose its conscience. As soon as Naboth had been stoned to death for a crime he had never committed, Jezebel urged her husband to go and take possession of the vineyard.

An Unexpected Response

At last, God's patience ran out. Ahab's appalling abuse of power had brought his sins to their fullness. At this crucial juncture the Lord sent for His most experienced prophet, and entrusted to him the strongest word he had yet been given against the wayward king.

If Elijah had once fled in terror in the face of Jezebel's threats, he would do so no more. The Lord showed him exactly what the king had done, where he was, and the terrible doom that awaited him.

We know Ahab well enough by now to be able to predict how he ought to have responded to Elijah's challenge. We would have expected him to run back to Jezebel, 'sullen and angry,' a spoilt child crying, 'It isn't fair.' But it wasn't like that at all. Something unexpected happened. At long last it dawned on the king's dulled conscience that it was beyond the realms of coincidence that Elijah should confront him at the precise moment when he was about to set foot on his new property. Ahab was overcome by the realisation that God knew all about the murder he had sanctioned.

Never one to do things by halves, Ahab tore off his royal robes and went about in sackcloth, in full view of his subjects. He was too distressed even to eat. Gone now was the arrogance with which he had strutted through the land. Gone too were the threatenings and the flattery, and the Lord looked on the abject figure of the repentant king with mercy. It is one of the most moving moments in the Elijah narrative. For the first and only time, God gave Elijah something good to say about the king:

> *'Have you noticed how Ahab has humbled himself before Me? Because he has humbled himself, I will not bring this disaster in his day, but I will bring it on his house in the days of his son.'*[4]

Ahab and Elijah were never to meet again. The prophet's task was done, and Ahab would end his days a sadder, but wiser man. His conversion does not appear to have been radical enough to have curtailed the activities of his wife, however, let alone to put right the many wrongs he had done to the household of God. It was, perhaps, a conviction of sin Ahab experienced, rather than an infilling of divine love.

Partial though Ahab's repentance was, it sufficed to postpone judgement on his family line for the immediate future. Nevertheless, each of the dreadful woes Elijah had foretold against the house of Ahab came to pass in the years immediately following the king's death. The consequences of the evil he had set in motion would live on far beyond his own reign.

The Perils of Greed

It was greed which proved Ahab's downfall.

Of all sins, covetousness is perhaps the most impossible to satiate, and the most difficult to overcome. The illusory quest to find happiness through riches has caused untold misery through the centuries. Solomon, who was better placed than most to understand this, sounded a warning to all generations:

> *'Whoever loves money never has money enough, whoever loves wealth is never satisfied with his income.'*[5]

Nelson Rockefeller, one of the richest men in the world, was once asked how much money he would need to feel really happy. His sobering answer? 'Just a little bit more.' *People who want to get rich fall into temptation and a trap,'* lamented Paul. He went on to depict the love of money as the root of all kinds of evil.[6]

May the Lord deal with any lingering tendencies to covet in our own hearts!

The Prophetic Calling

The Elijah narrative is exceptional in that every time the Lord commanded His prophet to do something, he did it straightaway. He was in every sense, an outstanding man of God, who fulfilled tasks that only a prophet could accomplish.

In one sense, times have not changed. God still works through a prophetic people who are seeking to follow the leadings of the Holy Spirit. Our nation has long nurtured a relative abundance of Bible teachers, but the Church is more effective when there is also a prophetic dimension.[7] If the Church in Antioch included prophets, as well as teachers, in the ministry team, then why shouldn't we?[8] In some cases, prophets will bring insights for the Church, or for specific issues, or even for the nation. More commonly, however, the Lord will simply use prophets to bring His word to the people in our fellowships, to help the Church grow in the beauty as well as the knowledge of God.

So significant is the ministry of a prophet, that the actual moment of commissioning of many of the biblical prophets is recorded for us.[9] Such men were love-gifts from God, for even when the message they brought was a hard one, it was still God's mercy and kindness to show people how things really stood.

When the Lord brought Israel out of Egypt, it was His intention to raise up a nation which would be a demonstration to the world of what a righteous society could be like, when it lived under the rule of God. In this plan, the prophets had a vital role to play.[10] At times of crisis, it was the word of the Lord through the prophets which, again and again, saved the nation from its enemies.[11]

Although the age of the biblical prophets is over, the Lord invites – nay instructs – His people to be eager to prophesy.[12] The testimony of Jesus is still the spirit of prophecy.

> *'When He, the Spirit of truth, comes, He will guide you into all truth. He will not speak on His own; He will speak only what He hears, and He will tell you what is yet to come. He will bring glory to Me by taking from what is Mine and making it known to you. All that belongs to the Father is Mine. That is why I said the Spirit will take from what is Mine and make it known to you.'*[13]

In His great task of restoring His bride, and bringing in His Kingdom, God is raising up a people to make Himself known in our land; perhaps a New Testament equivalent of a prophetic nation.[14] But let us not be narrow in our interpretation of what the prophetic ministry should consist of. I believe in watchmen who are concerned for their professions as well as for their Churches or their geographical regions. It is my privilege and joy to work with musicians, whose music reflects what is happening in heaven, and brings the presence of the Lord close to His people. Wise is the Church which recognises and nurtures those who have particular anointings, whether it be for the Church, their profession, or the wider community.

How can we tell when someone is being raised up for the prophetic ministry? In the first instance, we will recognise an above average ability to feel issues deeply – and who then turn these feelings into prayer. As we have already seen, much of a prophet's principal work is done in secret, going to God on behalf of men, as well as going to men on behalf of God. Secondly, we do well to be aware that prophets are almost always trained and tested through strange twists and turns in their life, together with extended periods 'in the wilderness'. These are necessary to make the person mature enough to exercise the prophetic ministry safely.

It is not always easy to discern whether these testings are proof more of God's favour than of human sinfulness. We need discernment. Calamities may equally befall a person because there is something seriously wrong in their life.

Testing the Vocation

Since discernment is the key, how can we recognise the false prophet we fear so much? This is by no means an easy matter. Even the disciples failed to realise what was going on in Judas' heart until the very end. One key is to look for the direction of the heart. Proud and stubborn attitudes can be an indication that something is seriously wrong.

It is wise, too, to heed checks in our spirit, especially if they are accompanied by warnings from other mature Christians. A false sense of loyalty to somebody (or our instinctive dislike of them for that matter!) can also make it harder for us to perceive when a person is in genuine error. The one thing we should not do, is to dismiss anyone lightly as being a false prophet. The best of us make many mistakes – but we learn from them. The false prophet, by contrast, refuses to heed warnings, and continually dreams up new excuses to prolong his delusion. Typically, these people are lone-rangers who brook no correction, unwisely supposing themselves to be superior to those who could help to set them straight. It is the work of superheated flesh and subtle demons to lead godly souls astray in such ways.

Commonly, the problem revolves around the sense of infallibility. Presumption is wishful thinking pushed too far – and false prophets are nearly always presumptuous. The Old Testament may incline us towards the concept of the Lord speaking in a fixed, authoritative manner. The temptation is to assume that we are likewise merely to become channels for the voice of God. But we are not 'taken over' by the Lord, as mediums are in séances. Our own character and personality are also important; God gave them to us, and He wants to express something of His own heart through them.

Moreover, when the Lord does speak to us, we should never assume that we know how or when God will bring what He has promised to pass, unless He specifically shows us. We must continue to seek Him for the details to unfold. Jesus taught so much on the need for perseverance, precisely because what God asks of us nearly always appears impossible at first sight. Giving birth to a vision requires great stamina!

Prophecies of blessing need to be prayed through to fulfilment, just as warnings need to be taken seriously in order to be averted. Most prophecies are best considered as being conditional on our response, rather than deterministic.[15] Jonah's doomsday words against Nineveh, for instance, appeared to present the city with an inescapable ultimatum, but when the people repented, disaster was averted.[16]

Why then do people make such elaborate attempts to predict the exact sequence of the end-time prophecies? We are simply not meant to know all the details in advance. Much still waits to be shaped by our prayers and repentance. Trying to work out ahead of time exactly how matters will develop is usually self-defeating. Even the exact sequence of the events concerning the Nativity or Calvary could not have been foreseen from the Old Testament prophecies.

Since it is only with hindsight that we can see how everything fits together, we should be wary of people who claim to know too much. There is a type of prophecy that is dangerous akin to divination in its attempt to predict the future. Man has an innate desire for an inappropriate knowledge of the future, and easily distorts such 'prophecy' to feed this deception. It fits in all too well with the western obsession to know, to plan and to schedule. Authentic prophecy, by contrast, is primarily concerned with revealing the heart of God.

There is a world of difference between checking our leading with others, however, and doubting that the Lord has spoken at all. It is a biblical norm that those who are called to the prophetic ministry will usually be asked to step out in faith, even to the point where they have to stake their all on God's ability to deliver them.

We must learn, at first hand, the absolute faithfulness of God. If we hesitate, it strengthens the hand of the enemy. As Derek Prince pointed out, God had a harder job persuading Jonah to fulfil his mission than He did in bringing sinful Nineveh to its knees in repentance!

Since the best of us is but a mixture, there will be many opportunities to doubt – especially during those periods when everything seems to be going backwards. After a particularly gruelling time of testing, Teresa of Avila remarked one day, with refreshing candour,

> 'If this is how you treat your friends, Lord, it's no wonder that you've got so few of them!'

Those who persevere beyond the testings will inherit the fullness of the Lord's power, and accomplish all the Lord has in mind for them to do – just as Elijah and Elisha did.

Prophets and Pastors

Few of us will be set apart to be prophets in the way that Judas, Silas and Agabus were,[17] but the Lord wants His people to respond to the inspired words that He speaks to His people. When prophets and pastors are working together in their complementary roles, clear objectives and goals can be set for the church and much wisdom be imparted into the life of believers.

This is why Scripture indicates that the callings are usually separate ones. If pastors have to both give and implement a word of prophecy, it can make the church over-dependent on their ministry. This can cause pastors much tension, too, as they seek to move the church forward into the new things God is revealing, while at the same time needing to nurture those who are finding the changes difficult to handle.

This call for prophets and pastors to work together in tandem is a test of our maturity. Human nature being what it is, such diversity is often perceived as a threat rather than as an asset. The problem is compounded by there being many self-appointed prophets about, who are prone to control others through their words. Equally, there are any number of overly cautious pastors, who find it difficult to welcome those who are moving in the genuine dimension of the Spirit's anointing.

Sadly, the Church has often proved too stifling a milieu for the prophetic word to flourish in. In the understandable concern to maintain order (to say nothing of the less worthy desire to preserve the status quo!) young prophets are all too often denied the security and the freedom they need in order to develop their ministry. Many who receive a genuine calling become discouraged by the lack of response, and gradually lose heart. Other churches, in which prophecy is commonplace, are in danger of not weighing the utterances properly. What God is really saying is missed in the excitement of the moment.

Prophets are the 'eye' of the Church, who help it find its true direction. They need to be welcomed, trained and accommodated. Their closeness to the Lord is invaluable for leading the people of God forward, especially in the realm of prayer and intercession. As John McLaughlin commented,

> 'The prophet's task is as much to bring the glory of intimacy with the Lord to the people of God, as to pass on specific messages from God.'

The fact that much of a prophet's most effective work will be in the unseen realms of prayer and meditation is no excuse for individualism. Even though the nature of the calling may cause them to remain slightly detached, prophets are only fully effective when they work in close co-operation with other ministries in the Church.

Exercising the Prophetic Calling

Prophecies express how God feels. They may reflect His love and His pleasure, or they may declare His grief and His anger. Elijah told Ahab exactly what God thought about him – and, on this occasion, the word of God brought about instant results.[18]

Concerning the way in which prophetic words are given, however, we should learn to judge a message more by its content than by the manner of its delivery. Prophecies can come complete with grammatical mistakes and still be of God; the message may be a true one, even if the way in which it is given reflects the character (or the nervousness) of the speaker.

Nevertheless, the way in which a word is delivered often has a bearing on whether or not it will be received. Given all the unusual manifestations we are witnessing at this time in the Body of Christ, it is as well to remember that the spirit of the prophet can, and should, be subject to the person's own control.[19] We do not need to rant and rage: the word of God will speak for itself.

The fact that there is much sub-standard prophecy abroad in the Church, does not mean that we should be afraid to speak out what God gives us to say. He wants us to grow in confidence, both in receiving and in handling His word. Logically, the Lord is more likely to entrust a word of great significance to a trusted member of the body of Christ, than to one who is consistently inconsistent. A great deal, therefore, rests on the character of the prophet.

As in other aspects of our lives, it helps to know our strengths and weaknesses, and to be honest about our track record. It is entirely possible to hear the Lord accurately in certain areas, whilst being far less reliable in others.

We are on safe ground if we say that prophecy usually serves to confirm us in a course of action rather than to direct us in some new way.[20] To say that prophecy must always be of a confirmatory nature, however, is to be less than faithful to the biblical picture. It would never have occurred to Elijah, for instance, to go and confront Ahab in Naboth's garden, any more than it would have crossed David's mind to leave his stronghold and go into the land of Judah, had not the word of the Lord summoned him to do so. Neither would the believers in Antioch have sent special gifts to their brothers in Judea, had they not been warned through prophecy of a forthcoming time of scarcity.[21]

We ourselves have benefited from such a directive word of God. While we were living as newly-weds in a flat, a friend told us that the Lord had impressed on him that we should go and buy ourselves a house. Largely because we were living by faith, I had never imagined that we would be able to obtain a mortgage. Spurred on by this word, we not only found a suitable house, but were led to the manager of one particular building society. He turned out to be an 'on-fire' Christian, who had read one of my books, and who was only too willing to help us secure a house. Considering that the landlord of the flat we had been renting died a few weeks after we left (which might have led to all manner of complications) we can never thank God enough for the gift of the house He gave us.

It cannot be overstated how careful we must be, however, in handling such a word. God does not take away our free will, and our words for each other must not do so either. Suppose that someone comes to us, claiming that the Lord has told them that we are to follow some specific course of action that had not previously crossed our mind. We would be most unwise to base our decisions solely on this one piece of 'guidance', unless the Lord confirms it unmistakably by other means.

We cannot do better than to bear in mind David du Plessis's advice, that we should submit a word of prophecy to someone for their testing, and preferably in the presence of someone who knows them well. Then, if anything is said which does not ring true, it is easier for them to shrug it off, just as they will be more confident of being able to accept an authentic word from God. This simple advice will help us to avoid much hole-in-the-corner foolishness.

Heeding the Word of the Lord

The words of the earliest prophets were committed to memory, so that they could be passed on for the benefit of subsequent generations. It is recorded of the young prophet Samuel that *'he let no word of God fall to the ground.'*[22] We are wise if we treasure the words that He speaks to us, perhaps by recording prophecies in shorthand or on tape, so that they can be properly weighed. This honours Paul's instruction that prophetic words must be heard, tested, and, if accepted, acted on.[23]

Paul encourages us to be eager to prophesy, and to do so in proportion to our faith.[24] I believe that Paul added this important proviso because he knew how easy it is for us to go beyond our faith, and to add our own conclusion or interpretation. We must stop speaking when the anointing lifts. To continue with our own thoughts and words merely takes away from what the Lord has said.

Few, if any, of us learn to prophesy accurately overnight. Since we are bound to make mistakes, both in our hearing and in knowing what to do with what we hear, it is vital that we overcome our fear of 'getting it wrong'. Grace and humility will help us to learn from our failures, but it will also help enormously if the leadership team is strong and mature enough to prevent wrong words from being acted on.

I have seen churches warned through prophecy of dangers which they have consistently failed to face up to. We are like the people of Ezekiel's day, who heard and approved the prophet's words, but did nothing to change their way of life. It is a terrible thing when God is forced to remove His blessing from an individual or from a church, yet it can and does happen.[25]

When the Lord has a corrective word to bring to His people, its effect will usually be to convict us of some particular area in which we have failed, rather than leaving us in a state of introspective confusion.[26] God told Elijah specifically where to go, and what to say to Ahab in order to convict him of his sin.[27] Prophecies which merely cause people to feel uneasy or condemned, however, are most unlikely to be from God.

Can you imagine the disaster it would have been if Elijah had brought such stern words to Ahab if God had not truly sanctioned them? Appalling though the thought may be, we do not have to look far to find modern-day parallels. Words have power when they are spoken, for good or ill.

No one is pretending that this is an easy calling. We will not always get it right. On the last night of the very first Conference I ever led, a man claimed he had words of knowledge for people to be healed. Because I felt the Spirit was leading the meeting in a different way, I did not release these words. Predictably, he accused me afterwards of quenching the Spirit. I went to the Lord in agony the following day. Had I got it all wrong? I found His answer both illuminating and reassuring. He did not say that I was either right or wrong, He simply said, 'I appointed you to be the leader of this Conference and I supported your decision.' What a responsibility!

Elijah needed great courage to confront men such as Ahab and Ahaziah – but the Lord would have seen to it that he would have felt still more uncomfortable had he not spoken out! Many of us can identify with Jeremiah, who compared the word in his heart to a burning fire which he could not hold in.[28] Fearful though we usually are, it is infinitely better to speak out the words that are forming inside. May the Lord win the battle between our embarrassment and His Spirit stirring within us, and so develop His prophetic calling on our lives.

Reflections

The prophetic ministry is all about the restoration of God's original purpose. Pray for the prophetic ministry to touch and impact every area of the Church's witness. I am told that the Greek verb 'to restore' can be used for the setting of a bone that has been broken, and for mending a hole in a net. There are many bones that need resetting, and nets that require mending in the Body of Christ today. Many have left the Church altogether because of misunderstandings which a loving visit might have cleared up.

Are there people the Lord would send you to? Wait on the Lord, for Him to give you wisdom how to approach them. Then have the courage to go in and rescue the prey that Satan has taken captive.

Pray too for the prophetic ministry to be wisely and safely administered in the Body of Christ – especially that prophets, pastors and musicians may work together in harmony.

Selah

> Lord, as You sent Elijah to Ahab, so I make myself available to go wherever You send me, to help or to challenge, even as I welcome Your help and challenge myself. Sharpen my ability to hear from You, and to exercise a prophetic ministry. In Jesus' precious name, Amen.

References

1. See 1 Kings 20:1–30
2. 1 Kings 20:42–43
3. Numbers 36:7 states unequivocally that a family inheritance should never be sold.
4. 1 Kings 21:29
5. Ecclesiastes 5:10
6. 1 Timothy 6:9–10
7. cf Ephesians 4:11–13; 1 Corinthians 12:28
8. Acts 13:1
9. Moses in Exodus 3, Amos in Amos 7, Isaiah in Isaiah 6, Jeremiah in Jeremiah 1 and Ezekiel in Ezekiel 2–3.
10. Hosea 12:10, 13; Jeremiah 23:28–29; Amos 3:7
11. e.g. 2 Kings 3:9–27; 1 Kings 22:7–28; 2 Samuel 2:18–25; 2 Chronicles 20
12. 1 Corinthians 14:1, 3–5, 19; Revelation 19:10. Nowhere is it assumed in Scripture that prophecy was purely for the old dispensation, or that it was to be confined to the early days of the Church. Such an interpretation suits only those who feel the need to explain the absence of the charismata in certain parts of the Church today. The Scriptures were never intended to dispense with the need to seek the will of God over specific issues.
13. John 16:13–15
14. cf Exodus 29:5–6
15. That is, automatically bound to happen.
16. Jonah 3:4–10; cf 1 Kings 20:29
17. Acts 11:27–28; 15:32
18. 1 Kings 21:21–24
19. 1 Corinthians 14:32
20. 1 Corinthians 14:3
21. 1 Samuel 22:5; Acts 11:27–30
22. 1 Samuel 3:19
23. *'Do not quench the Spirit; do not treat prophecies with contempt. Test everything. Hold on to the good'* (1 Thessalonians 5:19–21).
24. 1 Corinthians 14:39; Romans 12:6
25. See Ezekiel 33:30–33; cf 1 Samuel 15:26–27; cf Revelation 2:5
26. cf 2 Corinthians 7:10
27. 1 Kings 21:17–19
28. Jeremiah 20:9

Chapter 24

The Challenging Counterfeit

'Ahaziah ... sent messengers, saying to them, "Go and consult Baal-Zebub, the god of Ekron, to see if I will recover from this injury." But the angel of the Lord said to Elijah the Tishbite, "Go up and meet the messengers of the king of Samaria and ask them, 'Is it because there is no God in Israel that you are going off to consult Baal-Zebub, the god of Ekron?' Therefore, this is what the Lord says: 'You will not leave the bed you are lying on. You will certainly die!'" So Elijah went.'

(2 Kings 1:2–4)

Ahab was dead. His son, Ahaziah, had been crowned in his place, and the kingdom of Moab seized its chance to revolt against Israel. Ahaziah did nothing to put the rebellion down, for, like Belshazzar, he was intent only on his personal pleasures. The new king had learnt nothing from God's dealings with his father, but displayed all the worst excesses of both his parents.

One day, Ahaziah was leaning over the balustrade of his upper room when it collapsed. So severe were the injuries he sustained when he fell, that he turned to the ancient shrines of Canaan for help and guidance. To do so was a public denial of the Lord God of Israel. After all, Baal-Zebub was no more than the Philistine god of flies and the dung heap –

and it was only a few years since the Baals had been shown on Mount Carmel to be spectacularly impotent.

Elijah had been God's messenger to Ahab on three previous occasions. Now, as he neared the end of his life, the Lord entrusted him with a message to Ahab's offspring. The episode is less well-known than the confrontation on Mount Carmel, but it was equally as perilous a mission as his original visit to the royal court had been. The Lord gave Elijah the message that Ahaziah would die on his sick bed because he had turned from the Lord.

Elijah met the king's messengers, and the Lord's warning was passed on to the king. Rejecting the opportunity to have Elijah as his friend and adviser, Ahaziah responded by sending fifty of his crack troops to arrest the prophet. So far as he was concerned, Elijah was less a prophet than a traitor.

Ahaziah's commandos came across Elijah sitting on a hill – a fitting place, one feels, to find Israel's senior watchman. But they were unable to arrest him! Just as the mob which sought to do away with the Lord Jesus was inexplicably thwarted,[1] so these soldiers found themselves pitted against the power of heaven. At this supreme moment of danger, Elijah again turned his face to heaven and cried out to his Lord.

The Fire Falls a Second Time

> *'"If I am a man of God, may fire come down from heaven and consume you and your fifty men!" Then fire fell from heaven and consumed the captain and his men.'*
>
> (2 Kings 1:10)

Ahaziah had chosen to follow the Baals, and the Lord needed to preserve His servant's life. He did so in such a way as to demonstrate once more His holiness. The fire, which had previously fallen from heaven to destroy the sacrificial bull on Mount Carmel, blazed down again. All fifty of the soldiers were incinerated.

We can see so much of his mother, Jezebel, in the way Ahaziah handled this crisis. Rather than repenting in the face of so great a miracle, he rejected the word he had been sent and attacked the person who gave it. (There are many who do the same today.) Convinced that might was right, the king sent out a second force of fifty men – who met an equally sudden, fiery end.

We may safely presume that the third contingent of soldiers would have fared no better, had not the captain prudently thrown himself on Elijah's mercy. Here is a word that both touches and sums up God's heart. Studying the theme of mercy in a concordance is rather like looking up 'Smith' or 'Brown' in an English telephone directory!

As Peter would one day receive unexpected guidance to venture into the house of a Gentile centurion, so now the Spirit of God bade Elijah not to be afraid of this captain, but to follow him.[2] The Lord would be with His prophet as he made one last visit to the royal palace. Elijah delivered a final, uncompromising message to the king. Because Ahaziah had acted as though there was no God in Israel, and had turned instead to foreign gods, he would surely die. And so it turned out. Barely two years into his undistinguished reign, Ahaziah died, unmourned by all.

The Pagan Challenge

What are we to make of these twin examples of fire destroying those who oppose the work of God? We know, from the standpoint of life beyond the Cross, that we are called to pray for our enemies, rather than to call down fire on them – but we are also called to resist evil.[3] The Prayer Book uses words in its prayers against evil men such as, 'Abate their pride; Assuage their malice and confound their devices.' We may not often hear such language today, yet there are times when the proper prayer is undoubtedly not, 'O Lord bless so and so,' but rather, *'O Lord, confound Ahithophel and turn his counsel into foolishness.'*[4]

These are the moments when we are called to exercise the authority of the Lord in situations that would otherwise remain locked in the grip of enemy forces. This is a weighty work, and one that needs to be done corporately. Though we may feel sorry for the unfortunate soldiers (who were, after all, doing no more than following their orders) we would also do well to remember the threat that Ahaziah posed. Nothing less than the cause of God was at stake in the life of the nation. Elijah was not only in imminent danger of being put to death himself, he was also caught up in intensive spiritual warfare against a monarch who looked set to continue the worst excesses of the previous regime.

We can never afford to forget that our battle is with the unseen powers of darkness, and not with flesh and blood. Elijah's mission was to call the people back to the living God, and to show them that the vile Baals had nothing in common with Him. How relevant this is to our own generation! After all, if God were no different, or no greater than Baal, and all religions were equally as capable of leading us to God, then the Lord Jesus need never have died on the Cross.

The uncertainties of our own age, coupled with people's propensity to seek for hidden knowledge, explain in part why over sixty percent of all women in Great Britain regularly read their horoscopes. The popularity of occult activities such as palmistry, spiritualism, tarot cards, ouija boards, yoga and TM is self-evident. Such things corres- pond in many ways to the ancient shrines of Canaan. But why do people turn to these deceptive powers of darkness, when all we need to know about the future is to be found in the Bible?[5]

We have seen how God specifically commissioned Elijah to challenge Ahab about the murder of Naboth.[6] There comes a time when it is unacceptable to remain silent. Intimacy with God does not mean shrinking from confrontation – but we need God's wisdom in knowing how to help people who have become involved in pursuits that are leading their souls astray.

The Perils of Syncretism

Open any Sunday magazine and discover afresh the 'gods' our society worships. Study how they are presented to our consciousness. Idolatry, in one form or another, is every bit as active today as it was in the ancient world; it is simply more sophisticated.

Such idolatry should be evident to all – even though most of us accommodate ourselves more than we should with the prevailing spirits of our time. I am more concerned in this chapter with an altogether subtler threat to the purity of God's people: the watering down that occurs when elements of other faiths are taken on board, and assumed to be compatible with Christianity.

About a decade ago I came across a man who had heard his first word from the Lord. Quite literally, it was just one word: 'syncretism'. Only the other day I met a teacher who had had the same experience. Both had been startled to hear the Lord speaking to them so clearly: both had had to reach for their dictionary to find out what the word meant!

Syncretism is the attempt to blend elements of different faiths together under one banner. As such, it challenges the heart of the gospel, and the first of the commandments: that we are to love the Lord our God – and Him alone – with all of our hearts. We can be sure the priests in Elijah's day encouraged the thought that the ideas and traditions received from Baal worship would actually enrich their worship of Yahweh. Similar lies abound in our own day.

Rosalind and I were out walking one day, somewhere in the hills and valleys of Wales. We were meditating on a word the Lord had given us, that everything the Lord is doing in raising up 'Quiet' Retreat Houses for Himself would have a direct satanic equivalent. At that precise moment we saw two young men walking towards us, their faces aglow with the particular sheen of those who have found a mission in life. The reason soon became apparent when they shared that they were from a nearby Buddhist centre!

Who would have thought that such religions would gain so substantial a foothold in our country? Yet the unthinkable has occurred, and many theoretically Christian groups are now using elements of Sufi mysticism (a charismatic offshoot of Islam) and Hindu mantras in their meditations. (A mantra is an incantation to a Hindu god, and hence a direct invitation to the powers of darkness.)

It is a tragedy beyond words that people in the Church should feel the need to turn to eastern religious systems in search of 'enlightenment'. Why should this be, when Hinduism believes in a multitude of impersonal gods, who demand complete obedience, yet offer neither the forgiveness nor the practical help that the Christian enjoys? Nowhere do we see the spiritual bankruptcy of liberal Christianity more clearly than in this willingness to import eastern spirituality into its self-made vacuum.

New Age teachings are increasingly combining with the liberal views of many bishops and clergy in proclaiming complete untruths concerning the nature of Jesus. God is angry when men set up a rival god, and present him as being equal to Himself. This is not pique, it is a matter of eternal truth. Yoga for instance, is not of God. Such teachings have no place in the Church of God.

No matter that the spirit powers concerned take pains to portray themselves as beneficent, people who travel by this road are opening themselves to a terrible deception. As the Vatican succinctly warned,

> 'Sitting cross-legged on the floor thinking peaceful thoughts is not to be confused with the authentic consolation of the Holy Spirit.'

It was for such reasons that I wrote a booklet a decade ago entitled *The Hindu Challenge to the Church.*

A couple of simple analogies may help us to see how preposterous is the idea that we can tack on bits of other religions to our own, without doing harm to the whole. Suppose a man were to go to his local railway station to find out which trains go to London. He is delighted when the porter tells him that every train goes there. Just imagine his discomfiture ten minutes later on discovering that he is on a non-stop express to Glasgow! He had been wrongly instructed. All trains do not head in the same direction.

To give another example, if we are deeply in love with our husband or wife, how would we feel if someone else came along and claimed them as their own? This is effectively what is happening when people place Krishna, or other so-called deities, on a par with the Lord Jesus. Christ's claims about Himself stand as a litmus test for the Church as it prepares to enter the twenty first century:

> *'I am the Way, and the Truth and the Life. No-one comes to the Father except through Me.'*[7]

It is not, in a pluralist society, that we are to hold up our hands in pious horror, and shun those who have embraced such ways of thinking. One of the great joys of Rosalind's ministry is that it brings her into close contact with those who are involved in New Age practices. As a midwife she can come alongside people who, as a Christian worker, it would be exceedingly difficult to befriend.

Time and again she has been able to share and pray with such people, enabling them to experience the presence and reality of the Lord as she has done so. Nevertheless, we need to be extremely clear in our beliefs before venturing into such a field, lest we find our own faith being watered down.

The Universalist Deception

I am a great believer in the value of going to places that are consecrated to the work of the Lord. We will often discover a special sense of His presence there. Yet we must be on our guard, for universalism is rampant in such circles.[8] Where the balance of Scripture is lacking – for instance, where the love of God is emphasized to the exclusion of other truths – it is but the shortest of steps to embracing mystical elements from other religions. Especially the attractive idea that nobody will ever be excluded from such love.

Tragically, universalism has spread through many of the retreat centres in this country, assimilating in the process many dangerous teachings from eastern religions. Since there can be no other yardstick by which we are to judge spiritual experience than the Bible itself, I cannot warn too strongly that we are to have nothing whatsoever to do with Yoga, Transcendental Meditation (TM) or any other Hindu-based philosophy or religion.

Hinduism represents the complete and diametric opposite of the message of the Lord Jesus Christ because it teaches that man has no need of a saviour. Sin, like all other matters, is regarded as a mere delusion. The ultimate goal of Hinduism is not to become one with our Saviour, who loved us enough to die for our sins, but to become one with ourselves, and so to realise our own divinity.

This deception has been furthered by the attempts of modern psychology to accommodate evil by synthesizing it with good. This is the lethal legacy of Jung's misguided mysticism. It has done incalculable harm, because it has caused many to attribute evil, in so far as they believe in it at all, to God, instead of to the devil.[9]

The Lord Jesus Himself never ceased to warn against deceptive influences. His language was blunt and to the point. Because He saw matters from God's viewpoint, how could He pretend that something displeasing to God was basically alright?

Almost every epistle in the New Testament is concerned, directly or indirectly, with this issue of false teaching. The apostle John, for example, wrote his epistles as much against creeping Gnosticism as to reassure young believers. The edges of God's love are sharp, not fuzzy like New Age thinking.

To cut a path through the vast swathes of the devil's fields of heresy, we can perceive that cults either add their own doctrines to and beyond Christ's teaching, or else they subtract from it. We can basically define them, therefore, as falling into two camps: Christ plus – and Christ minus.[10]

The Lord's mercy towards all who turn to Him is more certain than the rising of the sun, but we must not be fooled by the psychologists' assumptions that we are all right as we are. God decreed that it should be the Lord Jesus Himself who opened the door of heaven to all mankind, who should also be the One to tell us that hell is not a child's nightmare but a frightening reality.

The Lord does not desire the death of any sinner, but Scripture makes it plain that He is glorified by the overthrow of His enemies, as well as by the praises of His friends. True, the summary punishments of the Old Testament have been exchanged for long-suffering; the righteous and the wicked co-existing until, at the Last Judgement, the Lord Jesus makes an eternal separation. But virtually every one of Jesus' parables ends on this theme of there being such a separation. Subchristian tales of a blissful life for all after we die must therefore be discounted. We would have no need of a Saviour if there were not something we needed to be saved from.

The great error behind the New Age teaching that 'we need to get more in touch with our feelings,' is the supposition that our feelings are trustworthy. Why should they represent truth when our heart is desperately deceitful?[11] We are not made clean by the emotions we express, but by the blood of the Lamb. Such things need resisting, even as Elijah challenged the Baals.

These are aspects of seeing with God's eyes that I would rather have passed over. It is easier, and far more agreeable, to speak about God's mercy than of His judgement – yet this would mean being unfaithful not only to the Elijah narrative, but to the whole tenor of Scripture. If we, as God's children, have experienced something of His refining process, as the fire of His love burns up the falsity in our own lives, then society at large faces a stark and terrible judgement.[12]

It is not that we are to start thinking and acting defensively, as though we were constantly afraid of being deceived. Therein lies the path to paranoia. Yet we do need to understand the spiritual realities that are involved in a given situation, and take an appropriate stand.

Elijah himself emerges from this latest fray in a most favourable light. Here he is at the end of his days, as full of fire and vigour as he has ever been. He is standing where he has always stood, in the presence of the Lord, still bearing fruit in his old age. The world may be tempted to discard the over-sixties, but God does not. He counts many 'Elijahs' among the ranks of the OAPs – or Old Age Pray-ers as we might prefer to call them.

Reflections

We are called to contend for the faith, and to confront false doctrine and wrong behaviour. How would He have you reach out to friends and acquaintances who are caught up in New Age or occult practices?

Selah

Lord, we cry out to You to expose counterfeits and deceptions wherever they are to be found. We pray for those who have been taken in to be rescued – especially for those who no longer believe that Jesus is the only Saviour.[13] We pray, too, that You will keep our own hearts free from deception. In Jesus' name, Amen.

References

1. Luke 4:28–30
2. 2 Kings 1:16; cf Acts 10:1–11:18
3. Luke 9:54–56; James 4:7; 1 Peter 5:9
4. 2 Samuel 15:31, 17:14
5. Read Isaiah 8:19–22
6. 1 Kings 21:17ff
7. John 14:6
8. Universalism embraces the doctrine that all men will be saved.
9. This is not to reject all the helpful insights into human behaviour that certain branches of psychology can offer. We would particularly recommend the books Leanne Payne has published: *The Healing Presence*, *Restoring the Christian Soul*, *Crisis in Masculinity* and *Listening Prayer*. These are challenging and profound books, invaluable alike for the counsellor and for those wishing to deepen their life of devotion. All are published by Kingsway. Many have also found the publications by John and Paula Sandford life-changing: *Restoring the Christian Family*, *The Transformation of the Inner Man*, *Healing the Wounded Spirit* and *The Renewal of the Mind.*
10. Galatians 1:6–9; 2 John 8–11. It is significant that some of the world's most powerful religions – such as Islam and Mormonism – owe their origins to prophecies which purported to be from heaven, but which categorically fail the test of Scripture.
11. Jeremiah 17:9
12. 1 Corinthians 3:13; 1 Peter 4:17
13. Acts 4:12

Chapter 25

The Schools of the Prophets

'The company of the prophets at Bethel came out to Elisha.' (2 Kings 2:3)

Elijah might have been happy to spend the rest of his days in quiet devotion, but it was important to the Lord that he share the lessons he had learnt with others. In the decade that followed the mighty contest on Mount Carmel, Elijah and Elisha were rarely in the news, but they were far from idle. They used the time wisely, reviving the schools of the prophets.

These missionary centres, in Bethel, Gilgal and Jericho, exercised a considerable influence in the land. It had been Samuel who had first gathered about him the pious and studious young men who became known as 'the sons of the prophets'. We are permitted on several occasions to glimpse the spirit and faith that were at work in these communities, which clearly sought the spirit, rather than just the letter, of the law.[1]

These seminaries were in great contrast to so many today, where prospective pastors are pushed through academic courses that have no concept of spiritual warfare (and which therefore leave graduates inadequately prepared for the opposition they will encounter in their ministry). The emphasis in these schools would have been devotional rather than academic, being given over to the study of Scripture, prophecy and sacred song.

These schools were a sanctuary where the spiritually hungry could find instruction, comfort and peace. As such, they provide an early forerunner of the medieval monastic tradition. It was the goal of these communities to understand God's heart. It was from their number that the Lord selected certain ones to be His chosen seers and prophets.[2]

For us, too, there is a call to train believers in the spirit and power of Elijah; to understand the dynamics of corporate prayer; to teach people how to listen to the Lord and what to do with the words we receive from Him. In other words, to transform our meetings into encounters with the Risen Lord.

Music and the Prophetic Ministry

Central to these schools was the dimension of sacred song. In 1 Samuel 10:5 we find a whole company of such disciples playing instruments and prophesying. This aspect of providing instruction through psalmody is of greater biblical importance than most of us realise. Some years later, when the kings of Israel and Judah embarked on a joint campaign against Moab, the army ran out of water. When the king summoned Elisha, his immediate reaction was to send for a harpist. In the stress of the situation, and hindered as he was by the presence of an ungodly king, Elisha urgently needed to quiet his own spirit.

The gift of music paved the way for a wonderful deliverance of the Lord.[3] We have much to learn about the ways in which music can aid intimacy, reinforce intercession, facilitate healing and pave the way for us to hear a word from the Lord.

Henry Wadsworth Longfellow described music as 'the universal language of mankind.' Luther held it to be the 'art of the prophets, and the only art that can calm the agitations of the soul ... one of the most magnificent and delightful presents God has given us.'

There is enormous power when music combines with the Word of God. If we agree with the man who said, 'After theology I give to music the highest place,' then we should honour this in our meetings by affording plenty of time for prayer and worship. Instead of rigidly compartmentalizing our services, I would encourage you to make the effort to find ways to let worship, prayer and preaching interact and flow from one to the other.

The Lord and His people alike are longing for music that takes us beyond the happy-clappy into a true reflection of His longings and desires. Heaven is full of music, and our worship should express what God is doing, as well as who He is. As we have seen throughout this book, this will include an emphasis on mourning and judgement, as well as of celebration.

Ushering in the Prophetic Ministry

There are many today who are being called to devote themselves to the arts, in order to restore a prophetic edge to what was once, but no longer is, very largely the Church's own domain.

The Lord has *'redeemed us from all wickedness, and is purifying for Himself a people who are His very own, eager to do what is good.'*[4] As we saw in the chapter 'The Prophetic Ministry', the Lord wants us to catch a glimpse of the things that He is involved in, and to understand where it is that we should most direct our efforts.

For each of us this will be different. Many of us will be called to edify the Church, but some will be called to work primarily in the field of politics, or the arts, while still others will be called to attend natural disasters, either in terms of practical relief or through intercession. God loves to create new openings for the gospel, and to develop strategies way beyond anything we could have thought of by ourselves.

Whatever our calling, however, we can not accomplish it on our own. Jesus taught the Kingdom of God, rather than just personal salvation. We have found that special power is released when members of a profession or organisation come together to seek God's blessing. Who can say how much good has been done by groups of people gathering to pray for their schools, workplaces and communities? When I consider the fruit my friends have borne in the Musicians' Christian Fellowship (to name but one of many such ministries) it seems to me that there are many modern day schools of the prophets around. Elijah himself would have been proud of them!

Overcoming the Demonic

Most modern day schools of the prophets major on worship and prayer, teaching the body of Christ to enter deeply into the Lord's presence. They are also concerned to teach right perspectives on spiritual warfare.

This is important, because many Christians today appear to be more afraid of the rise of Antichrist, than they are looking forward to the return of our Lord Jesus. We must resist the demonic expectation that evil will rule the world. That is not to deny that evil is establishing itself in places where it has no right to be.[5] The enemy is a master propagandist, and he has long succeeded in securing landing-points for sin and wrong thinking, in the Church as well as in fallen institutions. We have only to look at the endless committees that discuss sexual as well as theological issues, and which often end up rationalising sin rather than exposing it.

Scripture teaches that *'the whole world is under the control of the evil one.'* Jesus Himself called Satan *'the prince of this world.'* We have to reconcile such statements, however, against the ringing declaration that

> *'The earth is the Lord's, and everything in it.'*[6]

Satan is the god of this world in the sense that the 'world' corresponds to the prevailing system of beliefs and ideas. This is the world order that he can manipulate. But Planet Earth belongs to the Lord! Delusion is Satan's primary characteristic, just as confusion is his middle name.

Many of us are quite unnecessarily afraid that we ourselves may be suffering from demonic influences. It is true that if we do not make the effort to hate and separate ourselves from unrighteousness, we unwittingly strengthen the powers of darkness against us – but it is most unwise to treat everything as being a demonic problem. The Lord's grace normally protects us from such things. Only if a Christian holds on stubbornly to something is there any likelihood of a demon being able to latch itself on to that habit (or pattern of unforgiveness) and make it his own. Most of the time the devil is like a snake with no bite – or like an empty gun pointed at our head. It still needs courage to believe we will not be bitten or shot!

Our first and most important spiritual weapon is repentance, for this takes away the point of access – the 'house' that we have built around our sin or habit. Living in the opposite spirit is usually more effective than rebuking such things openly. After all, sins such as lust, greed, hate and fear are primarily sins of the flesh, and must therefore be taken to the cross. Demons can fire the desires of the flesh – but you cannot cast out flesh.

This is where many make serious mistakes. Such Christians often take it on themselves to pray directly against Satan, thus addressing the devil rather than God. It can cause serious upset in the course of a prayer meeting when people start addressing the wrong person! As Leanne Payne reminds us,

> 'We are always to minister to God, and to practise His presence. It is only when we encounter demons, principalities and powers as it were in our path, that we are to speak directly to them and command them to leave.'[7]

To be involved in spiritual warfare is not a licence to focus on demons. If a Christian becomes too focused on them, he can, quite inadvertently, provide the enemy with a landing strip, and become embroiled in all manner of confusion and unnecessary warfare. Yes, there are sins that need addressing, not to mention confessing, but this usually has more to do with habit-breaking repentance rather than with demon-binding.

There is a call here for maturity. We can bring darkness into our lives if we pray in the wrong way. Just as our task is to release people into areas of service, rather than to control them, so we are not the ones who can control the powers of darkness. That is the Lord's domain.

Nevertheless, the Lord will call some of us to pray for the corruption that is hidden in the heart of the nation to be exposed. This is a work for the mature, and one which must be undertaken corporately.

Our prophetic task is always to prepare the way for the Lord – which means overcoming the high places that are in people's hearts and minds. These are what need challenging, as we pray for the release of the Holy Spirit's power.

Reflections

In what ways have you experienced the prophetic ministry in your life and calling? Is there anything specific the Lord would have you do – or be involved with – to make Him known in your profession or special area of concern? Ask God to show you how to pray.

Selah

> Lord, we pray that You will be glorified by raising up a Church which moves in prophetic dimensions; men and women who reveal You as You really are. May more and more of us serve You in such ways within our chosen fields and professions. We pray for many modern-day schools of the prophets! In Jesus' name, Amen.

References

1. e.g. 2 Kings 6:1–7
2. Amos refers in 7:14–15 to his calling as being an exception to the rule. The original word for prophecy meant a 'boiling or bubbling over', a 'spilling out' of the things of God that were on their heart; cf 2 Peter 1:20–21.
3. 2 Kings 3:11–20
4. Titus 2:14
5. You may find it heavy going, but *The Grave Digger File*, by Os Guiness (Hodder) illustrates this point, as, in fiction form, does *That Hideous Strength*, by C.S. Lewis. (Pan).
6. 1 John 1:19; John 14:30; Psalm 24:1
7. *Restoring the Christian Soul*, Leanne Payne, pp. 209ff (Kingsway).

Chapter 26

Translated to Eternity

'When the Lord was about to take Elijah up to heaven in a whirlwind, Elijah and Elisha were on their way from Gilgal. Elijah said to Elisha, "Stay here, the Lord has sent me to Bethel." But Elisha said, "As surely as the Lord lives and as you live, I will not leave you." So the two of them walked on. ... When they had crossed, Elijah said to Elisha, "Tell me what I can do for you, before I am taken from you." "Let me inherit a double portion of your spirit," Elisha replied.

"You have asked a difficult thing," Elijah said, "yet if you see me when I am taken from you, it will be yours – otherwise not." As they were walking along and talking together, suddenly a chariot of fire and horses of fire appeared and separated the two of them, and Elijah went up to heaven in a whirlwind. Elisha saw this and cried out, "My father! My father! The chariots and horsemen of Israel!" And Elisha saw him no more. So they went down to Bethel.' (2 Kings 2:1–2, 6, 9–12)

Elijah's life has been so full of symbolic importance that we might almost have expected his last minutes on earth to be replete with spiritual meaning. Like Moses before him, Elijah knew his mission was complete, and that the time had come for him to be gathered to the Lord.

There were to be no more power conflicts with corrupt kings, no more lonely vigils in the desert, and no more preaching to the schools of the prophets. Elijah, who had walked so closely with his God, would be taken, visibly, to heaven. Knowing that his hour had come, Elijah embarked on one final farewell visit to the schools he had been so instrumental in developing.

It has been suggested that Elijah's discreet efforts to leave Elisha behind at Gilgal stemmed from a desire to help him find a new framework for his life in the aftermath of the loss he was about to experience. It is equally probable that he simply wanted to be on his own. God often allows great spiritual moments to be witnessed by others, however, so that they can be recorded for posterity. Moreover, the Lord had something higher in store for Elisha than to be a member, albeit an honoured one, of the school of prophets.

Elisha had been called to be Elijah's successor: they had been constantly in each other's company for nearly ten years, and he fully intended to stay with his master until the end, so that he could inherit his anointing.

When the Lord Jesus knew that the time had come to face His Passion, He took care to make provision for those He left behind. On the eve of His suffering He promised His disciples the coming of the Holy Spirit – but He warned them that they would only inherit this, His ultimate gift, if they kept their eyes on Him.[1] It is a striking parallel with Elijah's desire to reward his faithful servant for his persistence. He asked,

> *'Tell me what can I do for you before I am taken from you.'*[2]

It was normal for a first-born son to inherit from his father, and Elisha, who had long seen himself as Elijah's true son, had no hesitation in asking that he might inherit something more precious than worldly wealth. Single-minded in his desire to continue Elijah's ministry, he dared to ask for the seemingly impossible: a double portion of the prophet's spirit.

There are those who seek after power for all manner of misguided reasons, but there was nothing selfish in Elisha's request. Knowing the needs of his day, he was willing to pay any price, provided he could be of service to his God. He knew that his very choseness would make him a particular target for the powers of darkness, and that his time would never again be his own. But Elisha had long since paid the cost for such discipleship, and he refused to be deterred.

Elisha had asked for a hard thing, and even Elijah could not be certain that it would be granted. It is possible for people to come to the edge of the Promised Land, yet still miss out through sin or negligence at the crucial moment. Moses did.[3] Only if Elisha witnessed his master being taken from him would that privilege be granted him.[4]

So it was that Elijah returned to the region he had been raised in around Gilead. God often gathers together the different strands of our life at the end of our days – just as He does at the conclusion of some particular stage of it. As the final stitches are put in place in the tapestry of our lives, we are able to make better sense of all that has gone before.

Chariots of Fire

Elijah's last day on earth was a long one. Together with Elisha, he walked the better part of thirty five miles as they journeyed first to Bethel, then to Jericho, and finally on to the Jordan. As the two of them stood by the river that God had miraculously dried up to enable the Israelites to enter the Promised Land, they realized that they needed an equally great miracle to be able to cross it in the opposite direction. What the Lord had performed some five hundred and fifty years before on behalf of the whole nation, He repeated now for the sake of His servants. The two of them passed over without so much as getting their feet wet![5]

I am wary of presumption, and tired of the false claims of certain 'faith' teachers, but none of these must be allowed to deter us from exercising real faith. Does not the next stage of the spiritual life always look impossible from the outside? I can remember wondering how any human being could possibly speak in tongues, or pray for the sick or prophesy. Yet what appears an awesome mystery one year may become an entirely natural part of our life the next. God is bringing His people into new and deeper levels of authority and anointing.

Suddenly, it happened! As they were walking along together, Elijah was drawn up from the earth in a chariot of fire, pulled by horses of fire in the midst of a whirlwind. It is one of the most glorious and breathtaking accounts in all of Scripture. It seems fitting that one who had always sought to stand before his Lord should end his days on earth without suffering the entanglement of death.

The episode foreshadows the still more glorious Ascension into heaven of our Lord Jesus Himself – although He had no need of a chariot of fire. It is, on another level, a picture of how the Lord will suddenly return to Earth. At the time of the restoration and conversion of Israel, He will appear again on earth in His glory; and His coming will signal the greatest and most glorious epoch yet in the kingdom of God.

In all the excitement, Elisha had kept his eyes on his master. Now he knew for certain the secret of Elijah's power, for he had witnessed Heaven's incomparably magnificent intervention. He immediately resolved to test whether he really had received the anointing. Would the waters yield to His command? Picking up Elijah's cloak, he smote the river. The waters parted and Elisha walked across for the second time that day.

The anointing was real! He really was Elijah's successor! From now on, Elisha would operate with a completely new degree of spiritual authority, and be regarded as the true leader of the schools of the prophets. Like Elijah, Elisha had experienced a long apprenticeship, and he was ready to cope with this astonishing level of anointing. Wherever he went, striking miracles and stirring displays of the power of God attended his ministry. Elijah's passing was not only the end of an era, but the transition to a new and yet greater work of the Spirit. How true it is that 'God buries His workmen but His work continues!'

Elijah's name means 'The Lord is my strength', or 'My God of Power.' Elisha's name likewise epitomises his ministry: 'My God is salvation.' Elisha would sow the land his predecessor had broken up by judgements with the seeds of righteousness and peace. When Elisha stretches out his hand, it is not to close heaven, but to bring down showers of blessing.

The Lord raised Elisha into a position of great strategic importance, whereby he could know both the heart of the Lord and have the ear of the king. Later on, when he was trapped by the Arameans in the city of Dothan, and in great peril, he would again experience the help of those same horsemen of Israel. He had no doubts about their power!

It is wonderful how the Lord overcomes our natural timidity, and makes us men and women imbued with the same spirit and power as these mighty men of faith. It has nothing whatsoever to do with self-confidence, but everything to do with His grace.

The Transfiguration Encounter

Only the Lord knows why Elijah was taken when he was. Likewise, only He knows when our own work is completed. The Lord sometimes calls anointed servants home relatively early in their life, perhaps to save them from becoming the centre of idolatrous admiration, or of being forced into a mould they had never been created to fit. Who knows:

perhaps there comes a moment when the soul becomes more valuable to God 'on the other side' than it is down here.

But let us take some time now to come apart and consider that wonderful moment when the Lord Jesus was transfigured before the eyes of His wondering disciples. For Elijah found himself present on that occasion too.

> *'After six days, Jesus took with him Peter, James and John, and led them up a high mountain by themselves to pray. As he was praying, the appearance of His face changed. There he was transfigured before them. His countenance shone like the sun, and His clothes became as white as the light. Two men, Moses and Elijah, appeared in glorious splendour, talking with Jesus. They spoke of His departure, which He was about to bring to fulfilment at Jerusalem.'*[6]

Here, if it were needed, is further evidence of how highly God rated Elijah. On the Mount of Transfiguration it was Elijah who was chosen, along with Moses, to shine like satellites of the sun in the reflected glory of the glorified Lord. Truly, they were worthy companions of a matchless saviour.

As often in Scripture, we find the place of prayer and encounter with God elevated above the everyday world. Moses and Elijah were far from alone in becoming acutely aware of God's grandeur when standing on top of a mountain. We know how much the Lord Jesus loved going into the hills and to the Mount of Olives to be with His Father. It is a practice we will do well to develop ourselves.

Used though His disciples were to following their Master from one adventure to another, it must have felt like a distraction from their real work, when Jesus forsook the crowds, and headed off up the mountainside. Often in the past, Jesus had longed to be in a solitary place, but had stopped to minister to peoples' needs, out of compassion for their hurts. Now, He was showing another side of God's heart. Can anything be more important for us than to be more in touch with heaven? Is it not those who have stood in the courts of the Lord who have most to offer the world?

The Lord knew exactly what He was doing. It was His intention to reassure His three favoured disciples of His real identity, to prepare them for the intense emotional turmoil they were about to go through. For a brief moment they would see Him as He really was – and they would carry that knowledge with them for the rest of their lives.

Many years later, Peter showed that he understood the real value of this mountain-top experience when he wrote,

> *'We did not follow cleverly invented stories when we told you about the power and coming of our Lord Jesus Christ, but we were eyewitnesses of His majesty. For He received honour and glory from God the Father when the voice came to Him from the Majestic Glory, saying, "This is my Son, whom I love; with Him I am well pleased." We ourselves heard this voice that came from heaven, when we were with Him on the sacred mountain.'*[7]

The encounter on the Mount of Transfiguration was foundational for Peter, James and John, as they set out to plant the Church of Jesus Christ. It was also further proof of the continuity of God's self-revelation. Not only earth, but heaven itself participated in this wonderful moment. The presence of Elijah and Moses proves that there was nothing about Christ's kingdom that was at variance with the life and teaching of Moses and the prophets.

Follow Me

Jesus says to us what He said before to another curious and thirsty generation: *'Follow me.'*[8] There are openings today for all sorts of people. As He taught and cared for the first generation of Christians, so He will for us as well. He is giving us the freedom to do the things He has called us to do, and He will remove all obstacles to make it possible for the work to be done.

We need never be hesitant for the truth. There is only one truth, and if we hold back in proclaiming it, the devil will be pleased. The Lord knows that we find the evil around us frightening, but the faith of a Christian remains on top of everything. The Lord Jesus has shared everything with us, even the riches of His life with His Father, and we must sacrifice ourselves for Him. Even if we feel as though we are getting little reward, we must keep going, and not give up. He will take the little that we offer Him, and make it go an astonishingly long way.

I love the episode that follows the Resurrection, when the Lord appeared to Thomas, to strengthen the faith of one poor disciple who was going through a fit of the doubts.[9] Shortly afterwards, the Lord called out to His dispirited disciples to throw their net on the other side of the boat.[10] It was an exact repeat of the earlier miracle of three years ago; His special way of encouraging them to continue following Him.

The apostles had no way of knowing, three years earlier, all the adventures, let alone the hardships, that awaited them. They were beginning to understand now. They were changed men. No longer full of grandiose ideas as to which of them was the greatest, but humble servants who would devote themselves to forwarding the Kingdom of God.

These words, 'Follow Me,' are, for us too, the beginning and the end of His message to us. He calls us to be in His company, and to consult Him before we act. Satan is the real enemy, not those who have been fooled by him. They can be saved. At God's leading we must be prepared to go out of our way to help needy ones; to take His word to those who are blind to His messages, so that they too can have sight.

The Lord is longing for revival to come to the world, and for Planet Earth to be a holy place. By every means we must do all we can to remove the blockages that stop men from seeing Him. His angels are full of energy. Countless thousands of people are receiving new life all around the world every day, even as Satan tears at the world in his final, but futile attempt to wrest it from the Lord before His glorious return.

The whole history of the Bible is of God taking hold of the spiritually hungry and filling them with His power. Out of the fires of this battle will emerge the bravest, purest church the world has ever seen. May He continue to take hold of us, and to lead us in the paths of an intimacy with God that is lived in the constant awareness of eternity.

The One who was there in the beginning will be there at the end; He is with us, and in us, always. May we be faithful to our Companion, and walk as a son or daughter of the living Lord, a prince or princess in His Kingdom.

Reflections

> *'No eye has seen, no ear has heard, no mind has conceived what God has prepared for those who love Him.'*[11]

Now you have come to the end of this book, take time to review all you have learnt. Remembering the command that came from heaven – not just to speak to Him but to listen to Him – sit for a while in His presence and enjoy a time of communion 'on the mountain top' with Him. For every difficulty we face He has a solution; for every challenge a way forward. What does He have to say now to help prepare us to go back down into the valley again?

Selah

Thank you, Lord, for drawing Elijah into Your presence, and for teaching us so much through his life. Thank You that the power of heaven is at hand to help in every situation that we face. Thank You that You have called us to shine in this world, and to share eternity with You in the next. I ask that You will allow us to spend the rest of our days in Your service, and to end them in Your company. For Jesus' sake, Amen.

References

1. Luke 24:49
2. 2 Kings 2:9
3. Numbers 20:8–12
4. 2 Kings 2:10
5. 2 Kings 2:8
6. Matthew 17:1–12; Luke 9:28–31
7. 2 Peter 1:16–18
8. e.g. Matthew 4:19, 8:22,9:9, 10:38, 16:24, 19:21; John 21:9, 21:22
9. John 20:17
10. John 21:6
11. 1 Corinthians 2:9